The School Board

The School Board

KEITH GOLDHAMMER

Associate Director, Center For the Advanced Study
of Educational Administration
University of Oregon

42027

The Center for Applied Research in Education, Inc.
New York

Foreword

The school board is an American invention which is necessary because of the decentralized educational system. The school board is practically unknown overseas, and where it does exist, it does not have the policy functions which characterize it in the United States. The school board grew out of the Board of Selectmen in the community in an early age when civil, religious, and school affairs were combined. In our small rural schools at an earlier date, and, to a lesser extent in one room schools today, the board serves as the administrator, pays the bills, hires the teachers, and purchases the supplies. In our cities that are medium and large in size, the board of education at its best has become a policy-making body with the superintendent being the administrator who recommends to the board matters for consideration. School board members are ordinarily unpaid and spend almost unlimited hours on the development of a public school program.

The state has legal responsibility for the school, but it refers most of this responsibility to the local board. People in the community therefore think of school boards as their representatives. They believe that it is the board member's function to effect the community will in the administration of local schools. As a consequence, a school board member may find himself in a dilemma over what the community wants and what the state requires. This dilemma has never been entirely resolved. Board members are expected to be promoters of public interest in education, and they are expected to be defenders and upholders of the basically accepted values of the community. When these values do not coincide with the professional objectives, friction is inevitable, and sometimes conflict results.

A board of education may be considered an appellate body to hear complaints and grievance when parents or citizens do not feel the professionals have given them adequate hearing. Legally, the board of education hires personnel and in theory has close supervision over them. The board, of course, must depend on professional administrators in large districts. The school board is conservator of resources and is a liaison between community and school. Perhaps one can summarize by saying that there are three dominant ways in which board members tend to relate themselves to the broader community: first, board members attempt to reflect the community will; second, they may hear appeals when an individual feels that his interests are being adversely affected; third, they act as the conservator of financial resources of the school district. Frequently, the school board is self-perpetuated and represents the best educated, the economically most comfortable, and usually the more politically conservative elements in the community. Since board members are elected, they are as individuals, almost invariably responsible to some group in the community. In some instances school boards represent special interests which have particular desires on the school, either with respect to activities, curriculum, or finance.

The development of policy making by the board and administration by the superintendent has not been without conflict. At its worst, superintendents feel that the school board can be a hindrance in carrying out the best interests of education for the children. In contrast, some popular writers have insisted that the superintendents exert control over the schools and restrict the independence of the elected school board member.

As the appointed officer of the board, it is the superintendent's responsibility to evaluate the effectiveness of the educational enterprise and the extent to which it is meeting the needs of the young people. It is his responsibility to inform the board of inadequacies that have been revealed. It is his responsibilty to advise the board of various alternatives of action with respect to the problems which confront them and to assist them in understanding the consequences for the community of accepting one or another of these alternatives. It is also his responsibility to execute policies which the board establishes and to inform the board of the extent to which effectiveness of the program is promoted or hindered by these policies. If the school board and the superintendent hold different concepts of how the school should be organized, conflict is inevitable. That there is so little friction is a tribute to both board members and the superintendent.

PAUL B. JACOBSON

Dean, School of Education
University of Oregon

The School Board

Keith Goldhammer

This is an outstanding book on the work, purpose, and functions of school boards. Although there are several books in the field, this one stands alone in that it has a solid research base. The author is thoroughly familiar with his subject and has been one of the individuals who has done significant research in this area.

The book traces the historical and legal foundations of the American school board. It develops school board and community relationships, deals realistically with the school board and superintendent relationships, discusses the social structure of the school and its relation to the school board, includes a fine chapter on how school boards conduct their business, investigates the motivations, the social status, and the political, social, and economic attitudes of the school board member, and then projects trends into the future to see what will happen to American school boards.

The book is written in a brief concise manner; yet, it does not deal superficially with these important topics. Practicing administrators, school board members, and interested lay people as well as teachers will find this book to be a very important source of information about school boards.

Dr. Keith Goldhammer is Associate Director of the Center for the Advanced Study of Educational Administration and Professor of Educational Administration at the University of Oregon. For a number of years he has been engaged in field research and has specialized in the school board.

DANIEL E. GRIFFITHS
Content Editor

Contents

CHAPTER I

The Historical and Legal Foundations
of the American School Board

The American school board is a distinctively indigenous inno-
vation. It has evolved from its initial function of supervising the
religious orthodoxy of the locally appointed schoolmasters to the
quasi-legislative and policy-making body for the vast educational
enterprises which are found in the larger school districts of the
United States.

The school board (or—as it may variously be called—the school
committee, the board of education, school trustees, or board of
trustees) is the governing board of the legal governmental entity
known as the school district. Since most of the fifty state constitutions require that the legislatures provide for the establishment of
a system of schools in the states, the legislatures have had to develop a means for the effective conduct of educational affairs and
the governance of public school programs. In most states, the pattern which prevails is that established in colonial times, particularly
in New England, for the delegation of the state's responsibility to
specially created, local subdivisions. These local subdivisions (or
school districts) exist for only one express purpose: to provide for
the maintenance of the public schools in the area subject to their
jurisdiction.

In establishing school districts, the legislatures have not relin-
quished their final authority over the conduct of the affairs of the
public schools. Most authorities on school law assert that within
the limitations imposed by the state or federal constitutions, the
legislatures have *plenary,* or complete, power over public education
within their respective states. Consequently, they establish school
districts by the enactment of certain laws which enable school districts to act in behalf of the legislatures in carrying out their constitutional mandate with respect to education.

Generally, the legislatures have divided the power to act between the people and the school board of the district. The people of the local school district may have such powers as the election of members of the school board, the determination of the amount of money that may be levied in taxes annually in support of the local schools, the levying of bonds for the construction of school buildings, the recall of school board members, and the change of school district boundaries. All other duties, responsibilities, and powers over education are usually reserved for the school board.

Hence, the school board is that agency of government created by the state legislature and given the legal power to govern the affairs of the local school district. It is the key agency in the management of the school district and has power to act in accordance with the mandates and authority granted it by the state legislature. In most instances it can act independently of the desires of the population, whose authority is more rigidly circumscribed than that of the school board. The nature and functions of the school board have emerged out of a long history of the endeavor of local areas to manage their own affairs and maintain some independence from central government.

Origin of the American School Board

The first steps toward the development of public education in the colonies took place in Massachusetts. In 1647, acting in behalf of the church, the legislature required all towns to establish and maintain schools, and it imposed a fine for failure to do so. The entire responsibility for the establishment and operation of such schools was left to the people of the towns, and the early schools so established were administered, maintained, and controlled by the citizens of the town through their town meetings. In time, specific responsibilities for the supervision of aspects of the schools were given to individuals within the community. As the town grew in population, there was a general tendency to remove some of the powers directly from the people and to give them to the selectmen of the town. At one time, for example, the law provided that the selectmen must exercise careful supervision over the characters of the teachers employed.

Originally, there was only one population center in each town.

Gradually, the population spread into the rural areas, and the children of the inhabitants who moved away from the centers were restricted in their school attendance. By 1700, the rural settlers had become so separated from the town center that they demanded some powers and privileges of their own. Butts and Cremin emphasize that sparsity, however, was only one factor which contributed to the decentralization of educational control. The backwoods people were usually religious dissenters or were recent immigrants from European countries. Their educational needs were simple, and they wanted to maintain their own religious and national heritages. Consequently, they wanted to conduct their schools as a means of resistance to the official doctrines, both civil and sacred, of the state.[1] Thus in the early part of the eighteenth century, after considerable conflict between the rural and urban areas of the town, the local school district was established with its own right to elect school trustees, to levy school district taxes, and to select a teacher for its independent school unit.

As the town gradually increased in size, its pattern of government had to change, since communities became too large for the town meeting to be both a governing body and a chief administrative agency for the schools. The transition from a form of complete popular control to a governing body selected by the people of the community to administer their schools was also accomplished through gradual stages. As the educational function was extended and became increasingly more complex, there was a tendency to separate the educational function from other responsibilities of the local community and create it as a completely independent—or, in some instances, an almost completely independent—branch of government.

As the population of the United States spread westward and settled in remote areas of the country and in isolated parts of each state, the settlers found the New England system of control over education advantageous. It appealed to them as consistent with their spirit of independence and desire to manage their own affairs apart from the dictates of a central governmental authority. It also appealed to them as a rational answer to the complex problem of administering a broadly diffused educational system in each of the

---

[1] R. Freeman Butts and Lawrence A. Cremin, *A History of Education in American Culture* (New York: Holt, Rinehart & Winston, Inc., 1953), pp. 97–100.

immense western states. The local school district and the local school board were ready-made devices for constituting educational authorities to attend to the state's responsibility for the education of its children in each remote hamlet as well as in its metropolitan centers.

Sources of School Board Authority

The school board, then, is a creature of the legislature, established for the purpose of managing the affairs of the school district. By reason of its position as the immediate authority over the schools in the district, the board of education is responsible for the making of decisions, the formulation of policies, the development of programs, the employment of personnel, the levying of taxes, the provision of educationally related services, and the management of the use of the physical facilities of the school district. This delegated responsibility is defined by statute, interpreted by the courts, and, in some instances, expanded by custom. The amount of authority and the freedom of action exercised by any school board varies from state to state.

As a duly elected or appointed body, the school board operates solely as an agency of the state and derives its power primarily from statutory law. Constitutional and statutory provisions define the degree and the range of powers of the board. Some states provide for very specific enumeration of limited board powers and others for very broad and general powers, with a large degree of variation between these two extremes in most of the fifty states.

There are five levels of control over the independent action of the local school boards and from which local school boards derive their authority to act in specific situations. These levels of authority are: (1) the state constitution, (2) legislative enactments (statutory law), (3) the rules and regulations of the state board of education, (4) decisions of the courts, and (5) societal demands.

Constitutional provisions. Each of the constitutions of the fifty states contains some provision for education. Generally, these provisions are very broad, and the establishment of specific laws for the operation of schools is considered a legislative function. Except for general constitutional restrictions, such as bills of rights or similar means for the protection of the rights of citizens, there is seldom any specific constitutional provision which limits legislative control over education. Local and state educational agencies are "creatures of the statutes" and, as such, they may be created or abolished by legislative acts. Any constitutional provision related to individual rights or imposing ministerial duties on the legislature takes precedence over statutory provisions.

Legislative enactments. The school board's powers and duties have been specifically defined as those that are expressly granted by the statutes. Court decisions and differences in the wording of the statutes of various states provide some basis for implied powers, although these are constricted by the framework of the statutes. It is recognized by authorities in the field that school boards are responsible to legislative control and can exert no powers outside of the provisions of the statutes.

The school board is recognized by the courts as a "quasi-corporation," functioning with general characteristics of an incorporated local governmental body such as the city. Its powers, however, are restricted to functions directly relating to education. Unlike the municipal corporation, home rule charters which would enable them to operate on a broad and permissive basis have never been granted to school districts.

The degree to which legislative control is exerted over the local school district is determined by the state legislature. At its discretion the legislature can maintain very close control, establishing what amounts to a state school system with major decision-making authority retained in its own hands, or it can grant broad decision-making authority to local school districts. Although most state legislatures have fostered the establishment of decentralized school systems, the trend has been toward increased state control, particularly evidenced in the recently adopted state constitutions of Hawaii and Alaska.

In the absence of statutory provisions granting broader powers, a school board is necessarily limited to the exercise of those powers expressly delegated to it by the legislature. Hence, in the state of Illinois the courts have ruled that "school boards may exercise no other powers than those expressly granted or such as may be necessary to carry into effect a granted power."[2]

2 *School Directors vs. Flogleman,* 76 Illinois 189. Quoted in Keith Goldhammer and Lloyd Cooper, "A Survey of the Definition of School Board Powers," *Oregon School Study Council Bulletin,* Vol. 4, No. 8 (Eugene, Oregon: The School of Education, University of Oregon, 1961), 13.

The legislature of New York, on the other hand, has provided a very broad definition of school board powers, declaring that each board of education shall have the power and duty "... to have in all respects the superintendence, management, and control of the educational affairs of the district, and, therefore, shall have all the powers reasonably necessary to exercise powers granted expressly or by implication and to discharge duties imposed expressly or by implication by this chapter or other statutes."[3]

As the creature of statute, the board of education is considered a corporate entity with legislative enactments prescribing both mandatory and discretionary powers. Remmlein states that the school board, by legislative enactment, is a quasi-legislative or rule-making body, a quasi-judicial or discretionary body, and an administrative or ministerial body, as the result of the mandatory, managerial affairs which it must conduct.[4] The school board must perform certain functions with respect to the maintenance of schools and the protection of the health and safety of pupils, and it must provide instruction in certain courses required by law. As discretionary powers, the school board may enter into contracts, acquire property, levy taxes, employ personnel, disperse school district funds, enact changes in the curriculum, provide general control over school affairs. In some of these matters school boards have greater authority than in others.

Rules and regulations of the state board of education. Legislatures have generally considered it their function to establish the broad outlines for the operation of public education and to leave the filling in of the specific details either to a state educational agency or to the local school board. The state agency is primarily known as the state board of education and has an executive arm (known as the state department of education) operating under the commissioner of education or under the state superintendent for public instruction. The powers of state boards are generally narrowly prescribed by the legislature. They establish rules and regulations governing the operation of schools within each state as well as prescribing courses of study and, to varying degrees among the states, prescribing standards which must be met by the school dis-

---

[3] *Statutes of the State of New York,* Section 1709.33.
[4] M. K. Remmlein, "Legal Status of Local School Boards," *American School Board Journal,* 125 (May–June, 1952), 25–27.

tricts in the maintenance and operation of their educational programs. Probably the greatest authority exercised by state boards of education is through rules and regulations governing the certification of teachers, the establishment of rules and procedures for the revocation of certificates, and the prescription of the courses of study which must be followed in local schools.

Legal interpretations. Two agencies exist for the purpose of making legal interpretations of statutes which affect the operation of schools. In most states the attorney general of the state is designated as an agency for interpreting the laws of the state for its political subdivisions, and such interpretations have the force of law until reversed by a court of proper jurisdiction. In New York this function is performed by the state commissioner of education; in California, the county counsel in each county interprets the law and binds each school district in the county by his decision. The other agency for the interpretation of the law is the courts, which may act upon suits brought either by other agencies of the state or by private citizens in order to seek a proper legal definition of the authority of school boards.

Legal interpretation of school board authority is necessary particularly as the result of the doctrine of implied powers. The powers with which a school board is vested are those specifically expressed by the statutes and those that may be implied from ministerial responsibilities imposed upon the board by statutes. The degree to which a school board may function under implied powers is limited by the decisions of the courts as final determinates. There is, however, some variation among the states in the extent to which courts are willing to contest powers of local school boards, and there is a growing disposition to interpret implied powers broadly. It is fair to conclude that the courts will generally permit a school board to exercise the following powers and no others: (1) those powers *expressly* granted in the statutes; (2) those that are *fairly* implied in or incidental to the power expressly granted; and (3) those *essential* to the accomplishment of the schools' objectives.

When a court decides that a certain action of the board exceeds its authority to act, whether or not the action is worthwhile, the school board is limited to a strict interpretation of the statutes and must confine its actions and areas of responsibilities to those indicated by the court.

Societal demands.   There has been a general trend in American society to delegate increasing phases of the child's educational development to the schools. Areas of responsibility that formerly were undertaken by other agencies, such as the church or home, are now acknowledged as the school's obligation. Over the years, society has demanded that the school incorporate, for example, additional educational programs, recreational activities, and special psychological and health services. Although there are instances in which the courts have restricted the school boards in their endeavors to extend the school program, school boards have—as greater demands for such programs have developed—either ventured on their own and justified their actions on the basis of implied powers, or legislatures have extended the board's powers to include these programs. In many states, liberally minded courts have broadened the doctrine of implied powers to permit school boards to incorporate into the schools' programs innovations desired by the local communities.

Summary

Emerging out of its simple beginnings, the American school board has become an important force in the continuation and improvement of public education. It is established now as a basic characteristic of local government. It is extolled by some as one of the last bulwarks of popular control over a vital social function, and it is criticized by others as an outmoded agency of government which restricts the full development of the educational programs required by contemporary society. Beyond the legal considerations under which it operates, it has developed a complex pattern of functions and characteristics which have made it a subject for both subjective polemics and empirical research.

CHAPTER II

School Board and Community Relationships

The legal nature of the school board and its relationship to the state poses a problem for the school board member as well as for the average citizen of the community who is interested in school affairs. Whom does the school board member represent? On the one hand, he is legally designated as an officer of the state. He derives his powers from its legislative assembly, and his role is interpreted as that of acting in behalf of the state in matters pertaining to the local administration of the public schools. On the other hand, he is elected by the people of the local school district in which he resides. It is certainly the presumption of the electorate that school board members are its representatives and that their functions are to effect the "community will" in the administration of the schools. The potentiality of a conflict between the state's interests in education and local aspirations for the provision of educational facilities and resources is well known. What, then, is the proper responsibility of the school board member when he finds himself in such conflict? Does he more properly represent the will of the state as a whole than the expectations of his neighbors who elected him?

The dilemma has never been, and probably cannot be, totally resolved. In part, it arises from the failure to define adequately the relationship of the state and the locality in educational matters. As long as the state is divided into subordinate jurisdictions, problems of the relationship of localities to the central authority will certainly exist. In part, the dilemma is the result of popular practice which has caused the people to become accustomed to claim for their own jurisdiction certain functions which are not clearly defined. In part, it is the result of the fact that education is close to the people of the community, and informal channels of communication and lines of authority inevitably develop as a result of the visibility of the problems with which local schools are confronted. In part, it is the result of the conscious effort of legislatures to maintain decision making with respect to education on the local level and to arouse local initiative in providing resources for education beyond the minimum required by the state.

Community Expectations of
the School Board Member

In spite of the fact that this dilemma has been recognized by many authorities, there has been practically no endeavor to study systematically the types of expectations which citizens of the community have for school board members. Some indications of expectations arise from other studies, however, and experience indicates some common attitudes which prevail, at least among a significant section of the general population.

Knill[1] has pointed out that certain events appear to augment public interest in education. These events are also correlated with an increase in the number of critical articles appearing in popular journals. Within the last decade there has been a significant resurgence of popular interest in public education and increased pressures upon public officials to provide programs which various persons in the community conceive as necessary to improve the quality of education.

In a study of public education in New England, Gross found a variety of pressures placed upon school board members and superintendents in order to develop the types of programs which various individuals and groups conceived as important for inclusion in the public school program. These pressures involved demands for new programs, demands for the removal of existing programs, and protests of various sorts, as well as special requests for favoritism in the conduct of the business affairs of the school district.[2]

Gross also identified the sources of pressures upon school board members and superintendents which included, among others, parents or P.T.A. members, teachers, taxpayers' associations, politicians, business or commercial organizations, the town finance committee or city council, economically influential individuals,

[1] William Knill, "Who Censure the Public Schools?" *Oregon School Study Council Bulletin,* Vol. 4, No. 9 (Eugene, Oregon: The School of Education, University of Oregon, 1961), 13.

[2] Neal Gross, *Who Runs Our Schools?* (New York: John Wiley & Sons, Inc., 1958), 49.

personal friends, the press, old-line families, church or religious groups, veterans' organizations, labor organizations, the chambers of commerce, service clubs, and fraternal, farm, and welfare organizations.[3]

On the basis of the types of pressures which Gross found placed upon school board members by their fellow citizens, he concluded that "a good many people think the superintendent and school board members in their capacities as public servants, should be private servants too."[4] He points out that the nature of the pressures indicates that they are more in line with seeking satisfaction for the idiosyncratic demands of various citizens of the community. Since these demands are frequently contradictory, the school board member could be faced with an impossible task if he were to attempt to accede to even a fair share of them.

Six particular roles which local citizens most generally expect of school board members have been identified. Not all of these, of course, are held equally by all communities or by all individuals within a community. But experience of professional educators and members of school boards indicates that these are the roles that citizens commonly expect of school board members. Any one role or combination of roles may be emphasized by the public and may vary for differing situations or sets of circumstances.

Promoters of the public interest in education.   Probably more than anything else, citizens of the community expect schoolboard members to be promoters of the public interest in education. With the increasing professionalization of the instructional staff, the public has come to believe that the public interest has been subordinated to the concerns of the professional educator, and the ordinary citizens find it increasingly difficult to have their point of view officially represented in the decision making that takes place. Their only hope for an adequate representation is through school board members who are responsive to the public interest through the decisions that they make and the control which they exercise over public education.

Defenders and upholders of accepted values of the community. In one of his studies, Goldhammer found that individuals were nominated for the board by particular interests because they would

[3] *Ibid.,* 50.
[4] *Ibid.,* 48.

represent the values which such interests held to be important for the stability of the community. In the community studied, a school board member was expected by those who supported his candidacy to attempt to have these values prevail in the public schools.[5] Special interest groups frequently make demands upon school boards and attempt to identify their particular set of values with the general values of the community. It is anticipated by these individuals that school board members will recognize the necessity for having such values prevail if the children of the school district are to be properly educated.

This particular expectation has grown in importance as communities have expanded and the values of American society have become increasingly fragmented. In the early days the teacher was close to the families of the rural communities. These families had an opportunity to know the teacher and to supervise his activities carefully, lest he engage in behaviors which were considered immoral or unseemly. Now that the teacher lives in a larger community and, outside of the classroom, is lost in the crowd, there is increasing fear on the part of many parents and citizens that he might represent values that are incompatible with the basic culture of the community and the best interest of the growing boys and girls who are enrolled in his classes. In times of crisis school board members are frequently told that the community looks to them to uphold those basic values of the community with which professional personnel are believed to disagree.

Appellate body to hear complaints and grievances. When problems arise, parents or other citizens of the community are forced to deal with teachers or school administrators. Frequently, it is necessary for educators to reject their pleas and to deny their requests. As taxpayers of the community and as parents of the children who attend the school, citizens feel that they must have an avenue open to them through which they can appeal adverse decisions and receive redress for presumed wrongs. A school board member is frequently contacted by citizens who register complaints with him about certain phases of the school's operations. Presumably, the school board member is expected by the citizen or the parent to investigate these complaints and to take action in behalf

---

[5] Keith Goldhammer, "Community Power Structure and School Board Membership," *American School Board Journal,* 130 (March, 1955), 23–25.

of the complaining party. The expectation is constantly present that the professional educator represents a diverse point of view and special interest in education but that the school board member is similar to the average citizen of the community. He is expected to understand the citizen's point of view and to be willing to take action to redirect the educator in behalf of his fellow citizen.

Close supervision over professional personnel. Closely related to the previous expectation is the anticipation that the school board should maintain a close watch over professionals to see if their actions are contrary to the public interest or if their values are incompatible with the dominant values of the society or community. The average citizen expects the school board member to have some special means by which he can appraise school personnel and keep informed with respect to the methods of instruction or the types of decisions which are made. It is anticipated that the school board member will be able to select personnel who are competent to perform the various functions within the schools and to assume the necessary responsibilities. It is also anticipated that the school board member is in a position to require that educational personnel conform to community wishes.

Conservators of resources. Probably one of the most important expectations which people of the community have of school board members is that they will restrain professional or other employees of the school district who are likely to be unreasonable in their demands for the augmenting of school expenditures. Fundamentally, one of the expectations which is broadly rooted historically in the American culture is that the school board member will be a conservator of the resources available to the school and will seek to promote greater economy or reduction in school expenditures. Practically every school board member in the country has been confronted with a popular demand to cut the costs of education and has been reminded by citizens that he is expected to effect greater economy in school expenditures. Practically all of the statutes listing school board functions within the United States include responsibilities for the allocation of financial resources and the close supervision over expenditures. Those who have closely studied school boards have been impressed with the fact that decisions respecting the economic aspects of school operations appear to usurp the greatest amount of time at school board meetings, and practically all school board members who have been interviewed about their roles have stressed the degree to which they are responsible to the expectations of the community for effecting close control over the finances of the school district, endeavoring to secure greater efficiency and economy in operations.

This expectation has led to some difficult role conflicts for school board members who frequently find, after careful study of school problems, the need for augmenting the resources provided for education in order to assure its improvement in quality. As will be indicated in a subsequent chapter, board members are frequently more highly dedicated to the improvement of that quality than they are to economic restriction. There are many noteworthy examples of school boards and communities which place major emphasis upon procuring all the resources necessary to provide outstanding educational programs.

Promoters of individual rights and interests.   Gross and others have noted that many citizens expect to gain special favors through their acquaintance with school board members. Educators have frequently been reminded by parents who desire specific adjustments to be made for their own children, or by entrepreneurs in the community who desire a greater share of the school's business, that they are close to school board members and can appeal to the board to promote their interests in the event that educators do not satisfactorily attend to them. It is also expected that the school board members will be concerned about fair play in the operation of the schools and that they will seek adjustments through their close relationship with the administrators of the school district in the event that individual rights or interests are neglected.

How School Board Members
Relate Themselves to the Community

To understand the effect of the community's expectations of the school board, it is essential also to study how school board members appear to relate themselves to the community and whether or not, in their own definitions of their roles, they agree with the expectations which the other citizens of the community have for their positions. Research shows that school board members recognize that they are representatives of the community. It has been observed by several researchers that during the course of a single meeting the members of the school board may give expression in many ways to their interpretations of community expectations for specific aspects of the school's operation. It is a matter of some concern to school superintendents that the community and its expectations appear to be a more important reference group for school board members than a disinterested interpretation of what is in the best interests of furthering the educational program.

It is of particular significance that the evidence shows that board members, although feeling that they represent the community, generally represent rather narrow segments of the community. Goldhammer has shown that board members in the community he studied were active members of particular reference groups within the community and that their being on the board was the result of some organized attempt by their particular reference groups to have them elected. He had an opportunity to study present and former board members of a community over a period of some twenty years, and in each instance board members indicated that they had been encouraged to run for the school board in order to represent the point of view of some group within the community. The groups felt that their points of view were inadequately represented on the school board, and that particular educational or community values would result in the event that their positions were more adequately represented.

One board member represented the farmers in an outlying community of the school district. His constituents felt that their children were legislated against in the school activities program and that insufficient emphasis was placed upon the development of a well-rounded program in agricultural education. A second board member represented a more wealthy group of farmers close to town. They felt that the agricultural education program was socialistic in many of its characteristics and that it did not realistically prepare youngsters for their roles as managers of the larger farm operations which had to be maintained as rather sizable business ventures. Still another board member was a representative of a church group which felt that dancing was immoral and should be eliminated from the high school.[6]

One of the significant problems confronting the operation of the

---

[6] Goldhammer, "Community Power Structure and School Board Membership."

school board is the diversity of interests that may be represented. In one large city in which a school board is appointed by the mayor, for political purposes each school board member had to represent a different political interest group within the community. Under the circumstances, the mayor in selecting individuals could not disinterestedly select the best man for the job. He had to see that each religious, economic, and political group within the community felt that it had its particular representative on the school board.

As Leiserson has shown in his study of regulative boards, members who represent particular reference groups on boards are likely to use their positions to promote the values or interests of that particular reference group rather than of the public-at-large or of the function in which they had engaged.[7] Goldhammer also noticed that board members were less interested in the search for the most effective educational policies than of seeing the particular value orientation to which they adhered prevail in the educational program.

Although it is true that many board members see educational values as secondary to their other interests, it has also been noted that as they gain more experience upon the board they tend to become increasingly concerned about the educational programs; they adopt the public schools as a reference group superior to others with which they are also involved. This has frequently caused school board members to be criticized by other citizens who have not had the same opportunity to study the community's educational problems and needs.

Nevertheless, board members tend to look upon themselves as representatives of the community, and one of their primary functions is to direct and control the professional staff in accordance with the interests, wishes, and concerns of the citizens of the broader community. In this respect, they see themselves generally performing four basic roles in relationship to the community.

A pulse of the community. First, they see themselves as representing a pulse of the community. Among the board members that he studied, Goldhammer found that they felt that the superintendent or other members of the professional staff were to bring problems to them, and they would mediate these problems on the basis of

7 Avery Leiserson, *Administrative Regulation* (Chicago: The University of Chicago Press, 1942), pp. 130–33.

their understanding of what the community wished.[8] There were, however, several different interpretations of how the various members operated in this respect.

Some members believed that the board should determine policy on the basis of community needs and that the board members could keep in touch with the community and its needs by making themselves available to individuals and to groups that wished to contact them and promote some policy. Some board members constantly made themselves available to various citizens within the community and encouraged them to discuss school problems with them. Some of these contacts were solicited, although for the most part people approached the board members, since they knew that the members would listen and would report their sentiments to the board.

Other board members did not feel that this procedure actually secured the pulse of the community. They tended to feel that the result was nothing but listening to a few people complain about conditions of which they knew very little. Some of these board members felt that community contacts were important, but their point of view was that each member should listen to what was said and then make up his own mind as to whether or not a valid point had been made. These board members felt that they were elected representatives of the community because of what they stood for and that it was their responsibility to interpret the community's wishes in accordance with what they knew to be sound policy both for education and for the community.

Another group of board members said that they had been placed on the board because they represented the pulse of a certain group of individuals. When issues arose and they thought that some of their neighbors had a point of view that was pertinent, they would discuss these issues with them. Some felt, however, that they would do so only when their neighbors had enough information on the subject and enough understanding of the issues to discuss the matters intelligently. One board member in this category said that he wanted to represent the people and that he felt he could do so satisfactorily only by expressing unequivocally his own point of view. He did not feel that it was a part of his responsibility to

---

[8] Keith Goldhammer, "The School Board and Administration in the American Perspective of Government," *American School Board Journal,* 129 (November, 1954), 29–31, and (December, 1954), 29–30.

canvass the countryside on every issue that arose, since this would arouse community disputes. He was elected to represent a group of people because they had confidence in him, and he would have to settle his own problems in his own way.

Basically, all the board members studied felt that it was their responsibility to determine such policies as would help to maintain harmonious school and community relationships. They felt that a certain equilibrium had been established as a result of their representation of diverse interest groups within the community, and that they constituted a microcosm which duly reflected the points of view and aspirations of the citizens of the larger group of which they were a part.

A court of higher appeals. A second concept of board members' expectations with respect to the community is that of a court of higher appeals for citizens of the community who feel themselves aggrieved concerning decisions made by the members of the professional staff. Board members sometimes inform patrons that if they are not satisfied with the decisions of the staff, they can present their problems directly to the board. Since many individuals may want to avail themselves of this appeal mechanism but hesitate to come before the board, the board members with whom they discuss their grievance may personally report the issue and attempt to secure the board's decision either to uphold or overrule the superintendent or other staff members.

Aggrieved employees also are known to contact board members who show varying degrees of concern for their problems. Sometimes employees have bypassed their superiors within the organization in order to contact board members directly and seek relief from decisions which they feel are adverse to their particular interest.

Although it is sometimes difficult for members of the professional staff to accept this concept of the roles of the board members, in a democratic society it appears highly desirable that administrators of a public function be held accountable for their decisions and that an individual whose welfare is affected by those decisions should have some means for the review of decisions which he feels are not made in his best interests. In performing this role, board members may act as a safety valve for the schools, permitting individuals to express their concerns before major conflicts develop.

Conservator of finances. A third set of expectations for the manner in which school board members related themselves to the community was as the conservator of the finances of the school district. Goldhammer found that some members prided themselves for their business scrutiny of the school district's affairs and that they tended to a considerable extent to evaluate the superintendent on his ability to manage conservatively the business affairs of the community. In doing this, they felt that they represented the tax-payers of the community and were guaranteeing that individual wealth would not be dissipated as a result of careless management of school district funds. This point of view was particularly expressed by individuals who feared that the economy of the community was jeopardized by excessive school tax rates.[9]

Promoters of the educational function.   Recent research, to be reported in a subsequent chapter, shows that board members increasingly expect to be called upon to promote the educational function within the community. They frequently seek membership in order to assist in improving the quality of education and in interpreting educational needs to their fellow citizens while helping educators both to understand community desires for education and to obtain the resources required to develop an adequate educational program.

Summary.   Research and experience in the operation of school boards indicate that the following tend to be the four dominant ways in which school board members relate themselves to the broader community: first, as individuals who are attempting to reflect the community's will with respect to school policies; second, as a board of appeals to which individuals who feel that their interests are being adversely affected by the decisions by the professional staff can go for relief; third, as watchman of the financial resources of the school district to make sure that the community's wealth is neither needlessly dissipated nor carelessly handled; and fourth, as citizens who are primarily concerned for the improvement of the public schools.

Gross reinforces the concept of the community as the primary orientation of school board members. He points out that although the superintendents in his study reflected a greater obligation to teachers and other professional educators than did school board members, school board members reflected a greater obligation to

---

[9] *Ibid.*

local citizens than did superintendents.[10] On important issues, such as the designation of a particular tax levy, school board members are more likely than superintendents to identify themselves with the expectations of the community and to take into consideration the general needs of the community. Their particular point of view was found to be that a decision with respect to the allocation of money to education had to be placed in a perspective of general community demands involving functions and needs other than education. Gross concluded that it is likely that school board members see educational needs in the framework of a broad perspective, while professional educators look primarily at the educational need as an end in itself.[11]

The Relation of School Board Members to Community Influence

The existence of varying degrees of influence among individuals is a characteristic of all associational life. Although the phenomenon of power has been manifested in communities in various ways, centers of power or influence have been noted in almost all communities that have been studied, and powerful or influential individuals obviously control important social agencies. Where the power is highly concentrated, there tends to be a great deal of community stability, and leaders in almost all social functions tend to be related in some way to the power structure of the community. Where the power is more diffuse and where there may be various groups or individuals vying for positions of influence within the community, there is likely to be more conflict, and the leaders of various social functions may well represent different power concentrations within the community.[12]

Those who have studied community power structures have generally noted some relationship between the community power

---

[10] Neal Gross, *et al.*, *Explorations in Role Analysis* (New York: John Wiley & Sons, Inc., 1958), pp. 128–30.

[11] *Ibid.*, p. 132.

[12] See, for example, Floyd Hunter, *Community Power Structure* (Chapel Hill, N.C.: University of North Carolina Press, 1953); Robert A. Dahl, *Who Governs?* (New Haven, Conn.: Yale University Press, 1961); Delbert C. Miller, "Industry and Community Power Structures," *American Sociological Review*, 23 (February, 1958), 9–15; Roland J. Pellegrin and Charles H. Coates, "Absentee-owned Corporations and Community Power Structure," *American Journal of Sociology*, 61 (March, 1956), 413–19.

structure and the school board. In his study of Regional City, Hunter discovered that the members of the school board were second-line power figures; the top powerful group within the community did not become members of boards for the various social functions. They entrusted this responsibility to lesser figures who were dependent upon the most powerful group for achieving status.

Regional City was a major metropolitan center. Most power studies have been made of smaller communities, and in these studies the school board was more closely related to the central power structures. Vidich and Bensman, in a study of a small community in upstate New York, noted that the central leadership group, although small in number, occupied many of the available positions. In turn, the various members of this central leadership group served on the school board, and those who were not members assisted the school board in making important decisions which affected the community.[13] Vidich and Bensman also noted that one of the functions of the central leadership in this community was to act as a watchdog over the specialized leaders who had the technical competency and were professionally trained to perform the responsibilities of managing local functions. The school principal was one of the technical people whom the power structure felt they had to watch closely to see that his management of school affairs did not overbalance community life and, hence, infringe on other important social functions.

Although Hollingshead did not particularly study the influence structure of Elmtown, he nevertheless noted the degree to which the members of the school board were highly influential people within the community and tended to be associated in their general community life with individuals who also exercise a great degree of influence in other areas of concern.[14]

After reviewing a number of studies of the relationship of education to community influence, Griffiths concluded that:

> 1. The ultimate direction of the schools will be influenced to a great extent by the community power-holders.
> 2. Members of the board of education are generally either power-holders or representatives of power-holders.

---

[13] Arthur J. Vidich and Joseph Bensman, *Small Town in Mass Society* (Princeton, N. J.: Princeton University Press, 1958), p. 259.

[14] August B. Hollingshead, *Elmtown's Youth* (New York: Science Editions, 1961), Chap. 6.

3. The school administrator will be unable to exercise community leadership without the aid of the power-holders.

4. Since decisions affecting the community as a whole will be made by a small group of power-holders, the school administrator needs to know who they are and how they operate in order to assess public opinion.[15]

Goldhammer made a detailed study of the relationship of school board members to the local community power structure. He concentrated his attention on the particular problem of how individuals became members of the school board. He drew the conclusion that of the five-member school board in one particular community, two were members of the central leadership clique of the community; two were closely associated with this clique and considered "safe" for essentially all purposes; and one member was elected because a church group organized a campaign in his behalf. In the general apathy that prevailed during school elections, it was not difficult for an organized group to win the election through a write-in campaign, in spite of the fact that another member had been nominated by the most powerful group in the community.[16]

In a further endeavor to determine the degree to which central leadership figures outside the school board tended to influence school affairs, Goldhammer discovered that school board members sought advice from either the person who was considered to be the main leader in the central power clique or other members of the clique. It was apparent from the school board meetings which Goldhammer attended that on critical issues decisions were frequently delayed until school board members could consult with the central power figure of the community; then, when his recommendation was reported to them, the matter was rather quickly resolved.[17] Almost all the members of the school board, in their value orientations, were closely aligned with those of the identified leaders of the community, and school board members tended to hold as reference groups the same groups which were considered important by members of the central leadership clique.

These investigations have led to the suggestion that the central power group, or leadership clique, is a means for producing stability within the community and reducing the potentiality for con-

[15] Daniel E. Griffiths, *Human Relations in School Administration* (New York: Appleton-Century-Crofts, Inc., 1956), pp. 109–110.
[16] Goldhammer, "Community Power Structure and School Board Membership."
[17] *Ibid.*

flict. Griffiths offers the conclusion that "power is the cement that holds our society together."[18]

The situation is schematically illustrated in Figure 1. In this figure, it is seen that the community is an embodiment of certain stable policies, mores and values, sustenance patterns, a definite history, a patterning of social relationships, and an ecology, in which the people live and in which they are bound together by these other factors. Regardless of the size of the community, it is probably the function of the central leadership clique of the community to interpret these ingredients of the social life of the community for all areas of community life and to determine the degree to which the levels of aspiration of the community, with respect to various social functions, will be maintained. The clique also determines the amount of financial resources which may be allocated to the various functions within the community.

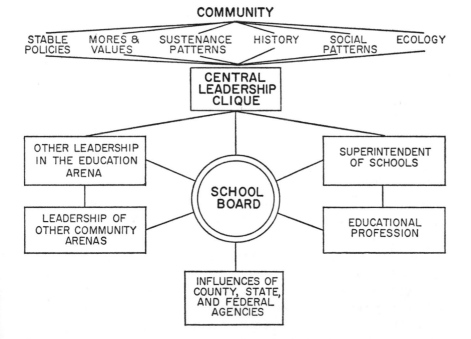

Figure 1. The relation of the Community and Outside Groups to the School Board

Source: Keith Goldhammer, "The Administration of the Community's Schools," *American School Board Journal,* 139 (October, 1959), 27–30.

---

[18] Griffiths, *op. cit.,* p. 105.

This central leadership group is a mediating agency. It takes an over-all perspective of community needs, aspirations, and resources, and it analyzes the relationship of various proposals to the maintenance or acquisition of stability within the community. It imposes its influence upon the school board as well as upon all other community policy-determining agencies. The school board exists as only one policy center within the community, and it has many relationships with others. Church councils, the city government, welfare agencies, and community councils concerned with the recreational function—all impose certain influences upon the school. If conflicts arise, then individuals within the central leadership clique may be called upon to mediate the differences.

In addition, individuals other than members of the school board have achieved leadership within the educational area. The P.T.A. president, a state legislator who has been active on various educational committees, or someone who has assumed a real interest in educational affairs may be such persons who help to mediate educational decisions before policies are finally determined. These people may act as a community force which either compels the school board to further action or restricts its complete freedom of behavior and decision making.

As seen in Figure 1, these are influences of the community that impinge upon the school board. There are, however, other influences which also are exerted upon the school board. Possibly, these forces may offset some of the community influences, necessitating that the school board take a view of its functions and responsibilities broader than the interests and concerns of the local community. It may be said that to a certain extent the community is a narrowing influence upon the school board, while other forces which operate primarily outside the context of the community are broadening influences. These forces include the concerns of the educational profession for the constant improvement of educational programs; the influences of county, state, and national educational agencies which may supervise or set standards for local programs and stimulate the development of special educational facilities and curriculums; social, political, and economic trends and problems which exist in the broader community and impose demands upon the schools; and the leadership of various groups and activities outside the community which may seek to promote their objectives through the use of the public schools.

The school board member is frequently enmeshed in a difficult dilemma in attempting to develop educational policies for the schools. He is a representative of the community and is probably closely aligned with influential groups within it. His welfare and that of the people with whom he is in constant association are dependent upon the nature of the decisions he will make. When the demands or restrictions of the local community are inharmonious with those of the broader community, he must decide whether he will maintain a provincial or a cosmopolitan outlook upon the schools' problems. He will be fortunate, indeed, if community power structures are oriented toward the broader view.

Griffiths suggests that the answer may lie in the endeavor of administrators and school board members to broaden the base upon which power exists in the community.[19] To the extent that more people are involved in decision making and to the extent that the community as a whole is represented in decision-making structures, there is the possibility of directing educational decisions toward solutions which will beneficially serve the vast majority of the people rather than a select group. This is also Hunter's solution to the restrictive influences of the power structure in Regional City.[20] The extent to which this is not done may provoke either popular apathy toward public education or actual hostility. Knill found in the community which he studied that the people who censured the schools viewed school officials as dominated by "influential people" in the community. They took little part in school affairs because they felt they were ineffective when they attempted to do so. Their hostility was released through bitter, and not always just, criticism of school practices and personnel.[21]

---

[19] Griffiths, *op. cit.,* p. 105.

[20] Hunter, *op. cit.*

[21] William Knill, *An Analysis of Attitudes Toward the Public Schools* (Unpublished Ed.D. dissertation. University of Oregon, 1960), pp. 78–79.

The Nomination and Election
of School Board Members

Very little research has been reported relative to the actual processes of the nomination and election of school board members. There are, however, two important aspects of how individuals become members of school boards which are worthy of exploration. First, there is a formal process of nomination and election in accordance with the laws established by the state for school board membership. Second, there is an informal process whereby individuals are actually screened for school board membership within local communities.

The formal process of nomination and election. Generally, throughout the country the only qualification for school board members is that they be qualified voters of the state and the district in which they reside. Eleven states have some educational qualifications; a few require character references; and three states require that school board members be freeholders. Four states require that a candidate for school board membership be either a taxpayer or a parent.

School board members are elected by popular vote in most states. In 33 states, all school board members are elected by popular vote, and in nine states most school board members are elected by popular vote, the exceptions usually being the larger cities in which the school board members are either appointed or nominated by another governmental agency. There are appointive boards in fifteen states. In the city of San Francisco, for example, the members of the school board are nominated by the mayor with the approval of the city council, but they are elected by the vote of the people. In view of a tradition of nomination of only one candidate for each position, the nomination has always been tantamount to election. In New York City, the board, under state law, is appointed by the mayor, and an amendment of a special legislative session in 1961 requires that he make his selection from a panel nominated by a group of designated citizens. In Philadelphia and Pittsburgh, the boards are appointed by the Court of Common Pleas. In Georgia, they are appointed by the grand jury. The Governor of Maryland appoints the board members in that state. Montana has some appointments by county commissioners; North

Carolina has appointments by the General Assembly; and Tennessee has appointments by the county courts.[22]

The process of nomination is a little more complex in many areas. In most states the members of the local school board are nominated either by petition, by a special nominating committee, or by floor nomination at an annual school meeting without reference to political affiliation. In a few states, however, local school board members run on a partisan ballot and are nominated by party caucuses. In still other instances, nomination is achieved merely by an individual's declaration of intention to run for the board. Whatever the legal framework may be, there is a more important consideration in how particular individuals happen to be selected for school board membership. This is the process of informal selection.

The informal process of nomination. Various studies show that communities tend (at least implicitly) to establish some qualifications for school board membership. Basic to the qualifications appear to be the individual's adherence to certain values and his exemplifying certain characteristics which influential people in the community hold to be important for the maintenance of community stability.

Informally, school boards tend to be closed groups which exert considerable influence over the nomination process. Because of their proximity to the source of authority within the school district and their knowledge of both coming elections and the laws relating to nomination procedures, incumbents are in a unique position to nominate either themselves when their terms expire or other individuals whom they think will make adequate members of the board.

One detailed study of how individuals become members of school boards showed that the process was usually initiated by a contact from a friend to inform the potential candidate that there was something wrong in the schools and that he was the person who could right the situation.[23] Although there was occasionally a contest for a position on a school board, generally there was only one nominee. Once an individual became a member of the board, he tended to serve several terms.

[22] Morrill W. Hall, *Provisions Governing Membership on Local Boards of Education,* Bulletin No. 3 (Washington, D.C.: Department of Health, Education, and Welfare, 1957).

[23] Goldhammer, "Community Power Structure and School Board Membership."

Conclusions that were drawn from this study indicated, first, that to a considerable degree the school board of the community studied was a self-perpetuating group.[24] In periods of stable school-community relationships, the only candidates that appeared were those who had been recommended by the school board. These candidates usually were the incumbents whose terms were about to expire. In periods of stress, a considerable amount of concern for the election of school board members was evident. It appeared as though the degree to which the board could maintain itself as a self-perpetuating entity was related to (1) the acceptability of candidates to the dominant power structure, (2) the general apathy of the electorate in school board policies, and (3) the strength of the power structure to confront challenges to it.

Second, although every board member averred that he was indebted to no group within the community, it was almost invariably true that his selection was the result of group action in his behalf. Each candidate was selected by some group which looked for the candidate to achieve certain specific ends through his school board membership.

Third, in many instances the school board candidate represented the power aspirations of some particular group within the community. When a church group wanted to control certain school policies, it endeavored to secure the selection of one of its members to a school board position. Similarly, groups in the rural areas within the community sought to control school policies through the election of dedicated members of their groups. On rare occasions when groups felt that school policies were inimical to their interests, there were lively contests for positions.

In most instances, studies have indicated that school board members were selected by some group within the community to represent them and their point of view on the board of education. In relatively few instances have individuals been found who, independent of any other community pressures, sought to run for the board. When independents without group backing run for election to the board, they do so because of some personal matter which they think they can accomplish by school board membership. Such

---

[24] See also Donald Faunt Wyss, *Certain Characteristics and Activities of School Board Members in Missouri* (Unpublished Ed.D. dissertation, University of Missouri, 1960).

individuals, however, rarely become elected and are frequently looked upon as eccentrics or fanatics. If they are elected, it is probably the result of some recurrent dissatisfaction in the school, and on such a point an individual usually is able to mobilize a group in support of him after he has declared himself for nomination.

As will be discussed in a subsequent chapter, informal process of nomination and election of school board members has resulted in the overrepresentation of certain socio-economic strata within the community. These groups are particularly concerned about the nature of the educational program and have the economic and educational qualifications necessary to represent their point of view adequately to the citizens of the community. Disadvantaged groups seldom, if ever, seem to be able to muster sufficient support to elect candidates. Studies made at the University of Oregon and at Stanford University indicate that these groups are seldom concerned enough about district elections or politics to engage directly in contests for school board positions.[25]

Relation of the School Board to Other Governmental Agencies in the Community

With the growing urbanization of American society, concern has been expressed frequently during the last fifty years for the improvement of essential services through the integration of local governmental entities. The local American school board has grown into one of the most extensive governmental enterprises on the local level and has, to a considerable extent, become independent of all other branches of local government. The expansion of services provided by city governments and by the public schools has placed the two in the position where they are now the primary competitors for tax revenues on a local level. The extension of the principle of home rule for municipalities has also led to the questioning of the place of education in the pattern of local authority.

Although educators have characteristically maintained that the

---

[25] See John M. Foskett, "Social Structure and Social Participation," *American Sociological Review,* 20 (August, 1955), 431–48; James R. Evans, *Identification, Behavior Patterns and Characteristics of Consistent Voters in an Oregon First Class School District* (Unpublished Ed.D. dissertation, University of Oregon, 1955); Richard F. Carter, *Voters and Their Schools* (Stanford, Calif.: Stanford University Press, Institute for Communication Research, 1960).

function of education is of such importance that it should be exclusively a function of the state and should be separated from the political control of the local municipal government, some educational functions have been delegated to the municipality. Legally, many instances exist in which cities and local boards of education are bound together. It has become characteristic to speak of *independent* and *dependent* school units. An independent school unit is one that is fiscally autonomous except for the constitutional or legal controls imposed by the people or the states. A dependent school district is one in which some other governmental unit has a measure of control over its fiscal affairs.[26]

Although many city school systems are not fiscally dependent upon the municipal government, they may receive several types of services from the city departments. Municipalities may be responsible for the conduct of school elections, the collection of school taxes, the holding of school funds, the auditing of school accounts, the provision of legal counsel, the employment of school personnel (other than the professional staff) through the civil service department, the purchasing of noninstructional supplies and equipment, the maintenance of school buildings, the planning of school sites, and the consultation of municipal architectural departments.[27]

In some states, legislatures have established quasi-governmental units which may supervise fiscal affairs of the schools on the same basis as they do the affairs of other local governmental units. In Oregon, for example, the Portland School District, along with all other tax-levying bodies of Multnomah County, must submit its budget to the Tax Supervision and Conservation Commission, which has the power to review the budget, call a public hearing upon it, and make recommendations to the levying body. It is further a responsibility of the Commission, upon the request of a body of taxpayers, to institute civil action against the members of the school board for the return of any money which may be spent in excess of the approved annual budget.

In other states, either legislative enactments or municipal home

---

26 W. G. Reeder, "Business Administration of Schools," *Encyclopedia of Educational Research*, ed. W. S. Monroe (New York: The Macmillan Company, 1952), p. 103.

27 Nelson B. Henry and J. B. Kerwin, *Schools and City Government* (Chicago: University of Chicago Press, 1938), p. 41.

rule charters call for various types of interdependencies between school boards and other governmental agencies on the local level. The courts have declared that in the absence of prohibitory provisions in the constitution, the legislature has the power to rest the management of the affairs of the school in the municipality. The Supreme Court of Wisconsin has ruled that "school affairs constitute a municipal function in cities and the Board of Education is merely a city agency, the same as the Board of Public Works."[28] The matter of complete dependence or independence appears to be one purely of legislative volition, and no basic concepts have come to exist over the entire country.

The most extensive study of community intergovernmental relationships involving school districts was that of Henry and Kerwin. In the majority of cities that they studied of over 50,000 population, they found that school elections were held at the same time as the municipal or general elections, and that the municipality was responsible for the supervision and expense thereof. In sixteen cities they found the mayor was an *ex officio* member of the school board, and in eighty-three cities they found that the city manager also acted as treasurer for the school district.[29]

Generally, the school district's taxing power was independent of that of the city, but in less than a fourth of the cities studied did the school district directly levy the tax. In the remaining three-fourths of the cities, this function was performed by city or county officials.

In approximately 80 per cent of the cities studied, the board was required to submit its budget to some other governmental body for review or alterations. New Orleans was required to submit its budget for approval to the State Budget Committee. In West Virginia, the city school boards had to submit their budgets to the State Tax Commissioner for review. All but first-class school districts in Pennsylvania had to submit their budgets for approval to the State Department of Education. In 40 per cent of the cities studied, the school boards had to submit their budgets to the municipal government, and in six per cent of the cases, this was only for filing or for consolidation with that of the municipality. In these cases, the mu-

---

28 *Ibid.*, p. 8.
29 *Ibid.*, p. 11–12.

nicipal government exercised no control over the estimates submitted by the school board, but in about one-third of the cities in the study, some control was exercised. In most instances, this was done only with respect to the total amounts of the budget.

There are some instances, however, in which city councils can change individual items in the budget. When they have not been guided by specific constitutional or legislative provisions which permit city councils to alter individual items, the courts have ruled that commissions or councils can alter only the total amount requested by the board of education. Henry and Kerwin's study is an old one, but it shows the extent to which school boards are dependent on other local governmental bodies. Very little change has actually been experienced in the two decades since their work was published.

The primary argument against the dependence of the school board upon other governmental units is that such dependence inevitably involves the schools in politics. Many political scientists have declared, however, that the schools are involved in politics anyway, and with the increasing rigor of supervision over once highly corrupt municipal governments, political affairs of the city are about as free of the adverse effects of politics as are school affairs themselves.

In 1961, scandals involving the administration of the New York City schools led, in a special session of the legislature, to the removal of the existing politically appointed school board and to giving the Mayor of New York City authority to appoint a new board only with the advice of a nominating committee of prominent citizens within the community. Many analysts of the situation interpreted the crisis as resulting from too much political interference in the local school system. Recommendations for improving the situation generally involved the independence of the board from further political control by the mayor and city council.

Although the issue of the pros and cons of dependence and independence continue, many instances of intergovernmental cooperation between school boards and other governmental agencies exist which enable a community to pool the resources of different governmental units toward the provision of particular services. Developments in the area of joint city-school district recreational programs, the joint purchasing of supplies and equipment by local governmental agencies, and the creation of school-park sites have led many observers to believe that much of the problem can be resolved without changing the basic structure of the governmental relationships of school districts.

CHAPTER III

School Board and
Superintendent Relationships

Authorities generally agree that the most important relationship related to the effective operation of the public schools is that of the school board and superintendent. The California School Boards Association has declared:

> The board works more closely with the superintendent than with any other staff member in the employ of the school districts. How effectively they work together determines in large part how well the program will be planned and executed. The board must strive to maintain a wholesome understanding of the relationship between itself and the chief executive for the schools.[1]

Stapley has stated that the most important single responsibility of a board is a selection of a superintendent of schools to act as executive officer of the school board in the administration of the community's educational program.[2] Legally, in most states the entire authority for the operation of the public schools has been delegated to the board of education. In all school districts except the very smallest, however, the accumulation of responsibilities and areas of operation makes it impossible for individual school board members to devote more than a very minor part of their time to school board affairs. In the rural schools of the nineteenth century the school board was presumed to be the administrative agency, and the law provided for the election of a school district clerk, who was responsible to the board both for the maintenance of the records and for the transaction of the board's business. In effect,

---

[1] Reprinted from *Boardsmanship, A Guide for the School Board Member, 1961 Edition*, H. Thomas James, ed., with the permission of the publishers, Stanford University Press, p. 48. © 1955, 1960 by the Board of Trustees of the Leland Stanford Junior University.

[2] Maurice E. Stapley, *School Board Studies* (Chicago: Midwest Administration Center, 1957), p. 3.

the clerk was the executive officer of the board in the small rural school district. Frequently, to administer particular phases of the program, school boards were divided into committees, and each committee assumed responsibility for the management of a particular phase of school operations. In such schools, the professional staff was composed almost exclusively of classroom teachers. In those schools which were fortunate enough to have several teachers, one was designated as head teacher, or principal, whose responsibilities in addition to classroom instruction involved disciplining the children and establishing some sort of contact with the school board in presenting requests for equipment, supplies, or the modification or development of rules and regulations.

With the improvement of communication and transportation in rural areas, consolidated school districts could be operated more economically and with greater educational advantage. With the passing of the small village school, there also passed much of the direct control of the local board of education. The problems of operation and administration became so complex that the local farmer, business man, housewife, or professional, although he was very successful at his own work, was no longer technically qualified to deal with all the problems that confronted the schools. A person trained for the job of school administration was required, and he became the advisor of the school board and the administrator of the schools when the board was not in session.

This growing complexity of organization resulted in a dilemma in the definition of responsibilities. The school board was charged with the responsibility for the administration of the schools, but this was a task that the members could no longer perform without competent professional assistance. They were, in essence, a board of amateurs and had to depend upon a professionally trained and skilled administrator to carry out the policies. The result was that although the school board was still delegated the legal authority over the schools, the members were to a great extent dependent upon the professional for information about school operations, instruction on legal matters, and advice on acceptable patterns of performance. The professional's skill, experience, and insight gave him a considerable amount of authority and power over the board.[3]

---

[3] Keith Goldhammer, "The Administrator and His Community," *American School Board Journal*, 134 (May, 1957), 35–36.

Needless to say, the transition has not been entirely without conflict. Many researchers have noted the degree to which the existence of ambiguity in the definition of the respective roles of the superintendent and the members of the school board has produced conflict between them. Hagen studied the patterning of school board members' roles over a period of twelve years in a single community. He developed two ratios as the basis upon which he could interpret his data: first, a *confidence ratio,* which was expressed as the degree to which the board members felt considerable confidence in the ability of the superintendent to interpret their policies adequately for the staff and community; and second, an *intervention ratio,* which was defined as the degree to which board members felt it necessary to intervene in the staff and community relationships of the school in order that their intentions be adequately represented. Hagen discovered that the two ratios varied inversely; as board members felt greater confidence in the superintendent, they were less likely to intervene in administrative matters and more likely to feel that their primary role as school board members was to support the superintendent and the *status quo* of the school district.[4] Gross found that the superintendents in the New England communities which he studied felt that the school board members constituted a major obstacle to the superintendents' executing their jobs in a professional manner.[5]

Throughout the twentieth century the popular literature on public education clearly indicates that the superintendent, or administrators in general, have been criticized because of the degree to which their professional positions enable them to exert a considerable amount of control over public education and, thereby, restrict the independence of the school board members. The dilemma appears to be compounded by the fact that the organization of the public schools is becoming increasingly complex and that the professional skills and competencies required for successful administration of the public schools are becoming more technical. Such a situation forecasts greater potentiality for conflict between school board members and superintendents.

---

[4] Arnold J. Hagen, *An Exploratory Study of the Patterning and Structuring of the Roles Played by School Board Members Through a Particular Time Sequence* (Unpublished Ed.D. dissertation, University of Oregon, 1955), pp. 161–64.

[5] Neal Gross, *Who Runs Our Schools?* (New York: John Wiley & Sons, Inc., 1958), p. 36.

School Board Members' Concepts
of Their Functions

Little research has been completed on how school board members view their particular functions with respect to the superintendent of schools. Hagen, as previously indicated, found that in Milltown school board members conceived of their role as perpetuating the *status quo* in the schools and alternately giving support to the present administration or emphasizing community values in the development of policies for the public schools.[6] Gross found that in New England most school board members felt that their jobs were political-patronage posts, and many of them sought election to the board to represent special segments of the community. These individuals had hazy notions of their jobs and spent a considerable amount of time dealing with trivial matters. They displayed little, if any, interest in the more crucial school problems such as curriculum improvement. Gross wrote:

> Some school board members act as if they, as individuals, had the right to make decisions, which is the prerogative of the entire school board. Some school board members act as if they, rather than the superintendent, had the right to administer the policy decisions of the board. Superintendents and school board members frequently disagree over their respective rights and obligations.[7]

Hollingshead found that in Elmtown the school board members comprised a homogeneous group. He found that the school board members represented very conservative elements of the community and were primarily concerned with two phases of their responsibilities: (1) operating the schools as economically as possible and (2) seeing that the teachers conformed both in the classroom and in their personal lives to the conservative economic, political, religious, and moral doctrines that were dominant in the local culture. The question of cost was uppermost in their thoughts, and educational innovations were carefully scrutinized to determine whether or not they were financially feasible. The school board members in Elmtown were primarily concerned about community values, and they were very much interested in holding the superintendent ac-

---

[6] Hagen, *op. cit.*, p. 94.
[7] Gross, *Who Runs Our Schools?*, p. 139.

countable for the economical operation of the schools and the instructional program, exemplifying those values which they felt needed to be conserved. Since the school board members had no important value differences with the superintendent, who found it congenial to work within the framework the board imposed, no conflict in perspectives arose.[8]

Vidich and Bensman found that the superintendent was recognized as "an alien expert" in educational matters. The school board felt that they were outclassed by their superintendent in respect to educational functions, and they were inclined to let him make the decisions on matters pertaining to educational policies. This was particularly true since the administrator had thought through the issues very carefully and had arrived at conclusions which were acceptable to him before he made recommendations to the board. The board, however, had two controls which enabled the members to keep the administrator in line with the values and perspectives which they deemed to be desirable. First, they had the power to fire and hire; second, they had control of the purse strings, which necessitated the administrator's maintaining rapport with their wishes.[9]

All the roles discussed in the previous chapter, both of the expectations of the community and of the individual board members, are pertinent in the relationship of the board with the superintendent of schools. To a certain extent, board members appear to express the opinion that they expect the superintendent of schools to bring into the decision-making setting the values of professional educators, based upon his experiences as a school administrator and as a person well-qualified to understand the educational implications of the board's decisions. They feel, however, that it is their function to keep him realistically attuned to the needs of the community and to assist him in making adjustments to community needs with which he would not be familiar.

The behaviors of the boards, as Hagen shows, vary to the degree that the school boards have confidence in the ability of the superintendents to make mature and professional decisions based upon this experience and preparation. At times, however, when they feel

---

[8] August B. Hollingshead, *Elmtown's Youth* (New York: Science Editions, 1961), pp. 123–25.

[9] Arthur J. Vidich and Joseph Bensman, *Small Town in Mass Society* (Princeton, N.J.: Princeton University Press, 1958), pp. 189–97.

that the superintendent has not made his professional decisions harmoniously with the expectations of the community (or with the particular reference groups within the community which they represent), board members feel that they have an obligation to perform in accordance with their appellate roles and intervene in behalf of what they consider to be either justice or the preservation of the community culture.[10]

As discussed in the previous chapter, school board members generally have considered themselves supervisors of the professional personnel, holding them accountable for the proper performance of their responsibilities. In view of the fact that board members lack the technical knowledge necessary to evaluate professional performance adequately, they tend more closely to scrutinize the degree to which the professional activity conforms to community expectations. The only representative of the professional staff with whom the board members are generally in close contact, however, is the superintendent of schools. Board members have to rely upon him for most of the information that they need about the schools, and usually they ask for his recommendation upon most issues prior to their making decisions. Consequently, he is in a relationship to the members of the board different from that of all the other professional employees of the school.

Current literature on educational administration is replete with concepts of what the relationship of the superintendent and the school board should be. Having been schooled in these concepts, the superintendent inevitably structures his relationships with the board at least in part by them. Experience in dealing with school boards reveals that the members are also considerably affected by these concepts, in view of the fact that they are the only models in the literature which are available and which carry sufficient "organizational logic" to enable the board to structure a satisfactory relationship with the large school organization for which they are responsible. Experience also suggests that board members are sincere in their endeavors to structure their roles properly, both in relationship to the needs of the community and to the supervision of the schools.

In one study, the board members of Central Forks believed that

---

[10] *Hagen, op. cit.,* p. 162.

there was a distinction between policy making and administration. They defined administration as "running the schools." It was more difficult to ascertain their definition of policy making, but it would probably be close to "making rules under which the schools will be run." Board members indicated considerable concern relative to the proper function of the school board in its relationship to the superintendent, and all attempted to justify to the researchers the ideas that they held on the subject. One board member believed that the board should pass on the recommendations of the superintendent, but that the members should not interfere with the way the superintendent wanted his staff organized. The member said that he wanted to see the board determine policy and assume responsibility for it. When critical issues came before the board regarding personnel, community relations, or disciplinary problems, he was always desirous of accepting the superintendent's recommendations, and he wanted the board to act on such issues only insofar as its actions would provide moral support for the superintendent. He felt that the board should be a buffer for the superintendent in his community relations since they were less vulnerable than he, and that the superintendent should not hesitate to use the school board in this connection in order to justify policies which were not popular with some groups in the community.

Another board member was very specific in his feelings that the board and superintendent should work together frankly and in complete cooperation on all issues. He would not separate certain items as the distinct province of either, but he did state that the board must act as a body rather than as individual members. He declared that it is a dangerous practice for the superintendent to have to work with individual members of the board on specific items. After the board established a policy, it was the responsibility of the superintendent to carry through with it.

A third board member did not want to be restricted by a definition of his responsibility in relationship to the schools and superintendent. He thought that the board should not try to run the schools, but he believed (and acted in accordance with this concept) that the board should hold the superintendent answerable to it for the manner in which the schools were operated. He believed that the board should set the major goals and policies, and that the superintendent should have personnel work out the details for the attainment of the goals. The board should be flexible and not make rigid rules, and it should hold the superintendent accountable in case his decisions were wrong. He considered the board's primary responsibility in relationship to the superintendent to be supervisory.

The most influential member of the Central Forks' board, however, had more difficulty in defining the relationship, presumably because he did not want to share influence with the superintendent and looked upon his position in relationship to the superintendent as somewhat competitive. In some instances, he believed in the separation of responsibilities; in other instances, he did not. He recognized the impossibility of the board's administering in place of the superintendent because the members could not have detailed knowledge of day-to-day operations; yet, he constantly referred to the fact that Central Forks was a small community in which the board could not relinquish its responsibility for the administration of the program. He wanted to see that certain policies were established so that regularized procedures could be employed. He wanted, however, to keep the situation fluid so that the members were involved in the resolution of many different issues in accordance with community values, rather than to restrict responsibility exclusively to the values of the educational profession. He persistently opposed the development of a set of written school board policies, urging that individual cases be brought before the board. Observers felt that his opposition was based upon the desire to see that the school board maintain careful control over all administrative decisions and actions.[11]

The research on school board role expectations clearly reveals that the human factor must be considered in the evaluation of any position. The perspectives which school board members have of their jobs are varied by the personalities, the goals, and the beliefs of the individual members. Because this is true, it is difficult to generalize about how a board functions, for the function of the board is a variable of the perceptions that the individual members have of their roles. If the member conceives of his role as that of the supervisor of the work of the administrator, the function will differ

---

[11] Keith Goldhammer, *The Roles of School District Officials in Policy-Determination in an Oregon Community* (Unpublished Ph.D. dissertation, University of Oregon, 1954), pp. 109–14.

from the situation in which the member conceives of his role as that of a buffer for the administrator between the professional staff and the community. The administrator himself will have to structure his roles differently. If the members' concepts of their roles differ considerably, it is apparent that some basic conflicts exist on the board and that these conflicts may impede the ability of the board to transact business.

School boards frequently attempt to keep their relationship to the superintendent fluid, thus preventing the development of a stable policy. This fluidity may sometimes be necessary because of the conflicts in role definitions expressed by various members of the board, but it must be recognized that this is generally an impediment to the effective performance of the school board's responsibilities. It tends to restrict the efficient and effective administration of the schools by the professional administrators.

School Board Members' Concepts of the Superintendent's Roles

Five particular role expectations for the superintendent of schools as held by school board members have been identified. These are generalized roles, and not all school boards or school board members concur in all the expectations.

Executive secretary for the board.   School board members generally hold that the superintendent should be an executive secretary for the board. Board members feel that it is their primary function to determine policies, while the superintendent should be responsible for putting the policies into effect and supplying the board with the information that it needs about general school operations. School board members feel that the superintendent should be an advisor to them and that he should keep them appraised of the implications and interpretations necessary to enable them to make wise policies, both with respect to the expectations of the community and on the basis of the knowledge and experience of the educational profession.

As executive secretary, it is the function of the superintendent to maintain adequate records for the board of education and to prepare the agenda for school board meetings. Boards expect the superintendent to assist them by bringing before the board those items which are essential for the board's adequate performance. Ideally, a school superintendent should see to it that the board has all the information which it needs in the event that a crisis occurs or any problems arise which will necessitate the action of the board. Obviously, this is a demand which cannot always be met.

As previously indicated, because the superintendent of schools possesses detailed knowledge about school operations and has been prepared to exercise the skills and understandings necessary for maintaining effective school programming, board members are considerably dependent upon him. To the degree that he keeps them informed and advises them appropriately, they will be able to act effectively. Board members, however, also have been somewhat concerned about the degree to which this possession of technical skill gives the superintendent too much power over them, for they believe that the superintendent's identifications are more closely with the educational profession than with the values of the community. The dilemma of the executive secretary is that although he is a part of the board group, he is also considered an outsider, exemplifying values to which the school board only partially subscribes. He is readily mobile and rarely a permanent part of the community.

This situation also creates a problem for the school board, for as long as it has to rely heavily upon its superintendent to operate the schools, to promote the values that the members hold to be important within the schools, and to keep the board adequately and impartially informed regarding school programs and activities as well as trends in education throughout the nation, the members are considerably dependent upon him for their successful operation. Whenever he fails in any respect in these matters, he can be charged with having withheld information which would conflict with the recommendations to which he had become committed. The school frequently has no alternative but to rely upon the superintendent, even though it may not always concur with the value orientations to which he subscribes as a professional educator.

Educational leader. School board members frequently refer to the superintendent as the "head of their school." They expect him to be the educational leader in the community, helping the community to interpret the educational program and endeavoring to educate the community regarding values inherent in school policies.

They expect him to know the difference between acceptable and poor programs and to be able to analyze whether or not every other professional employee in the system is providing the proper educational experiences for the children. They expect him to know the educational values of the various types of supplies and equipment, the types of building arrangements that will be educationally advantageous, and the actual educational needs that could be met through budgetary allowances. In fact, the superintendent is the board members' expert, and they want his first concern to be the education of the children. This is the job for which he is primarily trained. He is presumed to be able to interpret educational trends for the local community and constantly to evaluate the effectiveness with which the local educational program operates in accordance with the levels of educational aspirations held by the school board members and the community.

There are, however, some problems associated with the superintendent's adequate performance of this role. Since he is removed from the classroom, there is some question as to whether or not he is able to evaluate adequately the educational program and to advise the school board and community with respect to the adequacy of educational operations. The superintendent has too many responsibilities for the over-all operation of the schools to give either teachers or principals close supervision; yet, this is an expectation of his role, regardless of the size of the district and of the personnel on his staff.

Business manager. Because of the financial conservatism of many school board members, the superintendent is presumed to have considerable acumen and responsibility with respect to the careful business management of the schools. Sometimes board members look upon this role as being in conflict with his role as an educational leader. As the educational leader, the superintendent is presumed constantly to be promoting an extension of the educational program; as a conservator of finances, he is expected to operate a very economical school. Although in larger school districts (and even in many of the smaller ones today) there are specialized personnel to perform the technical job of business management, the superintendent is presumed to give direction to the business management of the schools and to scrutinize carefully the degree to which it is possible for the schools to operate effectively and economically.

Community leader. Although the superintendent is looked upon as an outsider, it is presumed by board members that he will be committed to the welfare of the community and will exemplify the values to which the community—or at least influential elements within it—subscribe. He is expected to accomplish this by being a leader in community affairs, promoting those civic enterprises which enable the community to maintain itself and to achieve patterns of operation that are harmonious with its value structure. Although board members generally maintain that they do not impose community obligations upon their superintendent, it is clearly indicated in the types of questions that they ask in employing their chief administrator (and in the job descriptions that they make for placement agencies) that they expect him to engage in many community activities, to interpret the school program to the community, and to reflect certain community values and activities in the type of leadership that he gives within the school organization. In smaller communities, in particular, the superintendent is highly visible as he performs his educational functions. Consequently, it is expected that he will engage in activities that identify him with the "right" social groups and the "right" social values.

Intermediary between board and staff. Since school board members look upon the superintendent as the person responsible for the transmission of their policies throughout the various echelons of the organization, they also look upon him as their contact with the rest of the staff. Since the literature of professional education warns against direct relationships between school board members and the members of the school staff, there is considerable feeling that the responsible school board will deal with the staff only through the mediation of the superintendent. Several studies have shown that this is a source of concern to school board members as well as to the superintendent. They recognize that the superintendent is a representative of the staff and has achieved his present position as the result of his educational experience in the classroom and as a supervisor or principal.

At the same time, they want to have their points of view adequately represented by their chief administrator, who exemplifies and upholds the values and perspectives which they deem to be necessary if the school is fully to represent the perspective of the community. Faced with this sort of dilemma, the school board and superintendent find it imperative to work closely as a unit and to attempt to understand each other's perspectives on all important matters. To the extent that this relationship breaks down, the school board develops, according to Hagen, a low confidence ratio in the superintendent and is very likely to attempt to intervene directly with the staff in order to see that its perspectives are adequately represented.[12]

The Superintendent's Concept of the School Board Roles

Just as school board members have certain expectations for the performance of the superintendent's role, the superintendent has expectations for school board members' performance of their roles. To a considerable extent, these expectations are influenced by the dictates of the educational profession, which has been greatly concerned about the relationship and which has prepared detailed statements of policy both for the consumption of school board members and for professional administrators.[13] Basically, the superintendent believes that the school board should be a policy-making body rather than an administrative body. Definitions of the distinction are difficult to make, and local interpretations are necessary. One might hesitate to attempt to describe all the variations in role definitions that are possible within the general framework of this concept.

Studies of superintendents' attitudes toward the school board reveal that superintendents generally believe that the members of the school board should, in assuming their positions, be prepared to make the sacrifices necessary for the performance of their duties. They should attend all school board meetings. They should attend

12 Hagen, op. cit.
13 See American Association of School Administrators, School Boards in Action, Twenty-fourth Yearbook (Washington, D.C.: The Association, 1946); American Association of School Administrators, School Board-Superintendent Relationships, Thirty-fourth Yearbook (Washington, D.C.: The Association, 1956); Charles E. Reeves, School Boards (Englewood Cliffs, N.J.: Prentice-Hall, Inc., 1954); Max S. Smith and W. Roy Smittle, The Board of Education and Educational Policy Development (Ann Arbor, Mich.: Edwards Brothers, 1954).

as many school functions as possible. They should define (if not defend) school board policies before community groups. They should be available to discuss with the superintendent problems of the schools at various times between school board meetings. They should be more than just passive observers who secure second-hand reports about the schools, and they should avail themselves of the opportunities to see the schools function directly, even though they do not interfere by having direct communication with the school employees whom they observe.

Superintendents feel that school board members should participate in activities involving professional problems outside the school district. They encourage board participation in administrative conferences, school board association conferences, workshops, and the like. They encourage professional reading among school board members, and they frequently subscribe to administrative journals for each board member. Through these devices, superintendents attempt to bridge the gap for school board members between community and professional values.

Superintendents, in accordance with the dictates of their literature, hold that the school board should determine major policies for the school district and the superintendents should administer the district in accordance with these policies. They feel that the school board should support them before the community and before their staffs in the interpretation which they give to school board policies. They feel, however, that there are two areas of operations in which the school board should act exclusively upon their recommendations and in accordance with their wishes. These areas are in matters pertaining to instructional methods and personnel. Problems related to instructional methods are considered by superintendents to be professional matters unrelated to public policy. The selection of sequences of learning activities, the adoption of textbooks, the development of course guides, and the determination of proper teaching devices fall within the jurisdiction of professional knowledge and go beyond the limitations of interested but, nevertheless, lay perspectives. Superintendents feel that interference in these matters constitutes an amateurish meddling in professional concerns.

The superintendents generally feel that personnel selection, evaluation, and recommendations for dismissal or retention constitute a power which they must have if they are to maintain effective and efficient organizational operations. Superintendents believe that the proper assignment and evaluation of personnel constitute areas of professional knowledge and responsibility, and that school boards are prepared neither by training nor experience to perform such services responsibly. Superintendents also feel that interference in employment by school board members is frequently an attempt to exert influence in behalf of special interests or friends and is done without knowledge of the degree to which educational values are promoted or hindered by such interference.

The superintendent assumes also that it is his fundamental responsibility to protect the members of the professional staff from arbitrary or capricious action on the part of representatives of the community or the school board. Consequently, by maintaining control over the appointment, assignment, and evaluation of personnel, he is in a position to assure that the criteria under which personnel will be evaluated are professional.

Policy Making and Administration

It is apparent that a significant problem exists with respect to the definition of the roles of the school board members and the superintendent in relation to policy making and administration of the public schools. The issue of policy making as the proper function of the board and policy execution (or administration) as the proper function of the superintendent has plagued both school boards and the profession of educational administration for a considerable period of time. Gross points out that school superintendents evaluate the effectiveness of board members in terms of the degree to which they conform to the expectations of the educational profession with respect to this definition of functions. The statements that are generally employed are indicative of the fact that no precise definitions are available.

In a study of the delegation of authority to Nebraska school superintendents, O'Connor found that smaller boards were inclined to retain more administrative functions than larger boards, and that all boards were more inclined to retain administrative functions in such areas as finance, school plant, equipment, organization, and control of employees than in the areas of the control of pupils and the curriculum. O'Connor suggests on the basis of his findings that the legislation of boards should deal with general statements of policy, leaving both the specific application and the procedures to be employed to the discretion of the superintendent. He feels that the proper definition of responsibilities can be made in terms of the school boards' acting in a legislative (law and rule-making) and judiciary (appellate) body. From this point of view, the board would not interfere with the executive functions of the superintendent, but would evaluate the degree to which the superintendent carried out the responsibilities which were given him.[14]

Donahue's findings in Connecticut are similar. He shows that contrary to the unanimous agreement of experts, superintendents tend to participate in the adoption of policies and frequently state that they even establish policies. In some districts, school boards also assume executive tasks which authorities would assign to superintendents. Connecticut's General Assembly delegated responsibility for education in school districts to local boards of education. The statute specifies 63 mandatory and 30 permissive responsibilities of school boards, but only nine statutory and two permissive duties of superintendents. Donahue found that in some school districts the boards of education were assuming the duties delegated by statute to the superintendents, and, similarly, superintendents were impinging upon the statutory authority and responsibility of the boards of education.[15]

In Illinois, Reavis also noted a tendency for board members to assume responsibility for the performance of administrative acts which they had already delegated to an executive officer. He concluded that an adequately functioning school board would be careful to delineate the areas in which it would act and those in which it clearly expected its superintendent to act.[16]

Pritchard found in a study of small school districts in Michigan that school boards were reluctant to delegate certain responsibilities

---

[14] Edward Burton O'Connor, *A Study of the Extent of the Responsibility Delegated to Nebraska Public School Superintendents by Boards of Education* (Unpublished Ph.D. dissertation, University of Nebraska, 1954).

[15] Edward Fredrick Donahue, *Identification and Differentiation of Responsibilities Assumed by Superintendents and School Boards in the Administration of the Public School System With the Evaluation of Existing Practices* (Unpublished Ph.D. dissertation, University of Connecticut, 1958).

[16] W. C. Reavis, "Relations of the School Board to the School Personnel," *American School Board Journal,* 116 (March, 1948), 32 ff.

to superintendents. As a result of their exercise of administrative responsibilities, they interfere with effective school operation and sometimes put the superintendent in an untenable position.[17]

In a study in California, Loutensock discovered that a dual administrative structure was created as a result of the board's duplicating the administrative responsibilities of superintendents or of retaining certain functions of administration for themselves.[18]

In a detailed study of the history of superintendent and school board relationships in Eugene, Oregon, Hines discovered that a clear designation of administrative and policy-making functions was not made until 1928. At that time, the superintendent was recognized as an executive officer of the school board, but his executive functions were significantly interfered with as a result of the perpetuation of a committee system by the board of education. In 1942, the superintendent succeeded in encouraging the board to discontinue the committee system. This resulted in the abandonment by the board of certain administrative functions which were then taken over by the superintendent of schools. In Hines' opinion, this was the first time that the superintendent was able clearly to act as the executive for the board of education.[19]

In a review of the changing conceptions of superintendent and school board relationships during the first half of the twentieth century, Plowman discovered that the attempt to make an adequate distinction between administrative and legislative functions occupied one of the most significant places in the literature of school administration during this entire period. It was his estimate that this problem was the source of one of the most important inconsistencies and ambiguities with respect to the development of sound principles of organization and administration in the public schools.[20]

---

[17] George S. Pritchard, *Duties and Responsibilities of School Board Members in Small School Districts* (Unpublished Ed.D. dissertation, Michigan State College, 1953).

[18] H. W. Loutensock, Jr., *Duties and Responsibilities of Officers of School District Boards* (Unpublished Ed.D. dissertation, University of Southern California), 1951.

[19] Clarence Hines, "A Study of School Board-Administrative Relationships: The Development of the Eugene, Oregon Superintendency, 1891–1944," *American School Board Journal,* 122 (February, 1951), 19–21; (March, 1951), 28–29; (April, 1951), 17–19.

[20] Paul Dearborne Plowman, *Changing Conceptions of Superintendent-Board Relationships in the First Half of the Twentieth Century* (Unpublished Ed.D. dissertation, Stanford University, 1958).

Walton has attempted to formulate a theory of educational ad-ministration on the basis of a distinction between the policy-making functions and the managerial, or executive, functions within the public school organization. It is his opinion that a bureaucratic officialdom now stands between the school board and the operating level of the school organization. The school board is the agency di-rectly responsible to the people, and as such it is presumed to establish the goals or objectives of the local public schools consist-ent with the requirements imposed by the state and by the levels of aspiration of the people in the local community. Because the new administrative class has proficiency in the techniques of both edu-cation and administration, it can exert power not only over the total operation of the organization, but also over the policy-making functions of the board of education.

Walton recognizes that educational administrators have realized the danger of their usurping both the public's concern as well as the professional concern for education. They have therefore endeavored to develop structures which would enable the public to participate in the formulation of educational policies to a constantly greater extent.[21] Walton holds, however, that the administrator must per-form his functions exclusively within the framework of educational purposes developed by the board of education. He states:

> In the last analysis, decisions about what should be done by the schools are lay decisions; neither the expert in administration nor the scholar has demonstrated any superiority over the layman in judgments about the purposes of education.[22]

Because of the very close relationship that exists between the school board and the administration, there inevitably develops a pattern of interrelationships that confuses any definition of the unique responsibilities for each. On the one hand, because of his superior knowledge of the educational program and administrative devices, the superintendent can usurp the functions of the board and restrict its effective decision making. On the other hand, be-cause the board has the primary responsibility for the employment or dismissal of the superintendent and the evaluation of his per-

---

[21] John Walton, *Administration and Policy-Making in Education* (Baltimore: Johns Hopkins Press, 1959), Chapter IV, p. 147.

[22] *Ibid.*, pp. 76–77.

formance, it can through this power force the superintendent to yield certain executive responsibilities to it.

The dilemma cannot be resolved except as some fundamental definitions are arrived at within the locality. These definitions are made on the basis of recognition of how the two positions can perform most effectively and in a cooperative fashion. This point of view is borne out by the evidence collected by Griffiths, who studied 24 selected school systems in two states. His study was based upon the assumption that school boards in those systems whose superintendents were rated as most successful would have delineated most clearly between policy making and administration. Instead, he found that there was actually very little distinction between the manner in which school boards reacted to his statement of issues, regardless of whether or not the superintendents were successful according to their ratings. He concluded that the best operational situations occurred when a spirit of teamwork and cooperation existed, regardless of the degree to which there was some overlapping of functions. Griffiths defines the situation as follows:

> This interrelation comes about because the board needs to know certain facts which only the superintendent has before policy can be made wisely. Likewise, in order to administer policy, the superintendent needs to understand all ramifications of the policy, and he can do so only if he is in on the development of the policy from the outset. In actual practice, in good school situations, it has been found that the superintendent normally supplies the evidence on which the board makes the policy. The board, in turn, is interested in the administration of the policy and checks on it by asking the superintendent to make periodic reports. In this manner, the board exercises control over the administration of the school.[23]

It is apparent that the issue of policy making and administration is not one that can be clearly delineated for all school boards in all situations. The evidence clearly indicates that cooperative relationships between the school board and administrator must be established in order to achieve a satisfactory level of performance within the organization and to make organizational policies clearly discernible to all individuals who must act in accordance with (1) the policies of the board and (2) the directives of their chief administrator. The diffusion of responsibility or actual conflict in responsi-

---

[23] Daniel E. Griffiths, *Human Relations in Administration* (New York: Appleton-Century-Crofts, Inc., 1956), p. 327.

bility inevitably results in low levels of performance and high levels of insecurity, tension, and organizational ineffectiveness.

The Structure of Relationships

What, then, is the most desirable pattern for structuring the relationship between the school board and the administrator? Regardless of any general principles about the relationship, operating procedures need to be established that are congenial to the occupants of the various related positions. Under the circumstances, there probably are few significant principles that are applicable in all situations. For the most part, each board and each superintendent should clearly state in written form the nature of the general policies under which he will operate. Writers in the field of educational administration appear to be practically unanimous in agreeing that written school board policies are essential to define the respective levels of responsibility between the school board and the superintendent as well as the operating rules which serve as guides to the conduct of other personnel within the organization.

A legal body that has been granted the authority to make decisions within a particular area of concern cannot delegate its power to perform services which it alone has the power to provide for the school organization.[24] By coming to terms with the problem of how each will perform in a given set of circumstances, the school board and the administrator can make adequate working definitions of their responsibilities. This will help assure that the efforts of each are directed harmoniously toward the accomplishment of the given ends.

There are certain guidelines that boards and superintendents may use to their advantage as they delineate their mutual areas of concern. First, it seems reasonable to draw a distinction between that which is purely a matter of public policy and that which is primarily a matter of professional knowledge and skill. It is certainly the prerogative and the unavoidable responsibility of the school board to make decisions in the areas which are concerns of public policy. Walton indicates these as being related to such activities as the provision of resources for the public schools, the establishment of purposes which will be served by the public schools, and the de-

---

[24] *Ibid.*, pp. 138–39.

lineation of the proper areas of operation in which the schools will engage. For instance, when a new field of study is to be introduced into the curriculum, it is a matter of public policy for the board to determine whether or not this is in accordance with the aspirations of the public and whether or not public funds should be expended for it.

On the other hand, it is within the responsibility of the school administrator and the other members of the professional staff to determine the breadth of the content of the course, the textbooks that will be used, and the teaching methods that will be employed. In clearly delineating areas of concern that are matters of professional knowledge and skill, the school board and the administrator will avoid acting on the basis of prejudice or misinformation, and they will maximize the extent to which professional knowledge, research, and experience are utilized in perfecting the educational program. In all these concerns, however, it is the responsibility of the administrator to keep the school board adequately informed so that it can evaluate the degree to which the professional staff is performing in accordance with the aspirations of the community.

If the board takes or fails to take certain action, the administrator's clear recognition of his responsibility to advise the board of the effects upon both the educational process and the community at large cannot be avoided. It is his responsibility to delineate for the board the alternatives involved in any situation and the consequences of their accepting one set of alternatives in preference to another. The board acts in matters relating to over-all policy decisions, while the superintendent advises; after the board decides, the superintendent executes. After he executes policy, the board, in turn, evaluates.

As the executive officer of the board, it is the responsibility of the superintendent to do three particular things:

1. It is his responsibility constantly to assist the board to evaluate the effectiveness of the educational enterprise and the extent to which it is meeting both the needs for education generally and the aspirations of the citizens of the community particularly. It is his responsibility to inform the board of inadequacies and of needs which should be met if the school is to achieve its purposes.

2. It is his responsibility to advise the board of various alternatives of action with respect to any of the problems with which the school district is confronted. It is his responsibility to assist the board in under-

standing the consequences for the community and for the public schools of its accepting one set of alternatives in place of another.

3. It is his responsibility to execute the policies which the board has established and to inform the board of the extent to which effectiveness of the educational program is promoted or hindered as the result of those policies.

CHAPTER IV

The School Board and the Social Structure
of the Schools

The Formal and Legal Relationship of the School
Board to the School Organization

Most educational practices are inherited from earlier periods of history. Undoubtedly, these practices were developed in response to some perceived needs which existed at the time of their development. Although conditions related to the operations of the schools have changed, there is a tendency to resist the modification of existing practices and structures or to alter accustomed ways of transacting the business of the school districts. Consequently, some legal practices and requirements persist which do not entirely accord with present needs of the schools. Such a discrepancy is readily apparent when one compares the legal role of the school board to its actual relationship to the total school organization.

Legally, the school board is in complete charge of the total organization of the schools. The *Oregon Revised Statutes* pertaining to education state: "Except where statutes are inconsistent with this section, district school boards shall have entire control of their district public schools and of teachers employed by the district."[1] Various other sections of the Oregon law give to school boards almost complete control over the operation of the schools except where limitations or obligations are imposed by specific statutes. In no place does the law recognize the authority of the school superintendent over the operation of the internal organization of the schools. Oregon law specifically recognizes the superintendent of schools only with respect to the granting of authority to the school board to employ a superintendent of schools and the desig-

---

[1] *Oregon Revised Statutes,* Section 332.110.

56

nating of power to the State Board of Education to specify the qualifications for certification for the office.

Similar legal provisions are present in the codes and laws of other states, although some states may give substantive powers to the superintendent to nominate personnel for appointment and to recommend further employment or dismissal. It is anticipated in the statutes of most states, however, that the school board will be the source of authority over the public schools, and that all decisions affecting the operation of the public schools must either be made by the school board or be subject to review and reversal at the pleasure of the board.

Even in the areas in which state laws dictate specific responsibilities for school boards, there is a tendency for the courts and legislatures to view these issues as guideposts, governing the school board's decision making. Hamilton and Reutter have stated that the operation of a local school system is so complex and local autonomy so deeply ingrained in the general legal pattern of school government that local boards are vested with broad discretionary powers.[2]

Legally, the school board employs the superintendent of schools and, under certain circumstances, dismisses him or fails to renew his contract when it expires. The school board also legally employs all school district personnel. Although in some states the superintendent is required to nominate school district personnel, in other states the school board can act upon the employment or retention of personnel regardless of the nomination of the superintendent.

Legally, the superintendent and other personnel act in the name of the school board in whom all authority for action reposes. In view of this fact, there is a tendency on the part of school personnel to justify their actions in terms of school board policies. It is not infrequent for a school patron to be told by a principal or teacher that the primary reason underlying certain decisions of school personnel is that such is in accordance with the requirements of the board of education.

School laws in many states still require that the school board

[2] Robert R. Hamilton and E. Edmund Reutter, *The Legal Aspects of School Board Operation* (New York: Bureau of Publications, Teachers College, Columbia University, 1958), p. 48.

make frequent inspections of the public schools. This, of course, is impossible in many large school districts in which there are so many schools that a thorough inspection would require the full-time employment of the members of the school board for several months of the year. Such a provision had, undoubtedly, good reason for existence when the schools were primarily rural and the only employed personnel, other than the custodial staff, were teachers with relatively indifferent preparation for their responsibilities. In those times the whole process of education was relatively simple, and the curriculum and methods of instruction and control were well delineated for the needs of a comparatively homogeneous community. But with the growing complexity of the school organization and the increasing professionalization of the certificated employees of the district, the school board is now put in a position of being the supervisor of the professional activities of a staff who are highly trained and, in most instances, competent to make decisions in areas in which the members of the school board are not.

Scholars of the legal relationships of school board members to the functioning of the school organization generally hold that there are two distinct types of authority which the school board exercises over the rest of the organization. The school board exercises certain *discretionary authority,* and it has certain *ministerial functions* which it must perform. Although it is not possible to make an entirely clear-cut distinction between the two aspects of the board's responsibilities, there are some indications of clearly delineated legal principles involved which can guide the work of the school board.

A discretionary power of the board is one which gives the board the power or the right to act in the event that it chooses to do so. There is no legal necessity to act unless the board considers that there are conditions which warrant its performance or which necessitate that it make a decision. In most states the school board is given the right to dismiss teachers. Regardless of what circumstances prevail, the board has complete discretion to act or not to act as it sees fit, as long as contractural rights are not violated. The school board, for example, is empowered to make changes in the curriculum, and it cannot be held either liable or responsible for the failure to do so, even though there may be strong justification for its acting. In some cases in which damages have accrued to

individuals because of the board's failure to act, or even of its acting in a fashion that may have been construed as negligent, the
courts have ruled that since the board was operating within the
discretionary powers granted to it, there was no legal liability of
board members for either failing to act or acting in a negligent
fashion.

Ministerial functions are functions which the law imposes upon
the board and which it must perform regardless of the presence of
any condition which, in the minds of the members of the board,
would indicate a desirability not to act. The school board, in most
states, must operate school for a designated number of days. If the
failure of the public to pass a tax levy restricts the amount of
money available for the maintenance of the schools, the school
board still is required to hold school in accordance with the law
for the designated number of days. In this instance, it is not clearly
delineated how they will be able to do so without funds. In some
states, even without a tax levy sufficient to provide the money
needed for operating the schools for the legal length of time, the
school board must operate the schools either by issuing tax anticipation warrants or by borrowing money against future tax levies in
order to do so. The failure of the board to act when it is clearly
indicated that the function to be performed is ministerial results in
the incurring of legal liability on the part of individual members of
the school board.

Garber reviews an interesting case that was passed upon by the
Supreme Court of Kentucky. In this case, a school board failed to
provide liability insurance, although the law granted the school
board the authority but did not require it to do so. The Supreme
Court ruled in behalf of the board; it held that if the statute had required the board to carry insurance, the individual members of the
school board would have been liable for injuries resulting from the
negligence of one of its employees. Garber indicates that in such an
instance the duty of the school board would have been ministerial in
that it involved no discretion. Since the statute simply permitted the
board to carry insurance, however, the board's failure to do so resulted in no liability to the board because the duty of the school
board was discretionary.[3]

---

[3] L. O. Garber, "How Liable Are School Board Members?" *Nation's Schools*,
62 (December, 1958), 64.

Hamilton and Reutter indicate that there appears to be a marked tendency for an increased amount of state regulations which mandate certain actions, or procedures, with which local school boards must comply. These include such requirements as the provision of various types of insurance covering the operations of the schools and protecting the public against liability, the provision of tenure, the requirement for boards to contribute to state retirement funds, and so forth. All these acts are compulsory, and in the performance of them the school board acts only as the minister for the state. In the event that the board fails to perform, individuals may have redress through the courts and may compel the school board to act.[4]

There are also acts in which the legislature has merely granted permissive authority to the board, expressing what appear to be a set of minimum standards or conditions under which the board may act. Such a law is interpreted as a guidepost, and the failure of the board to act does not give either employees or patrons of the school district the right to seek recovery from the board or to compel it to perform. As Roach has shown relative to teachers' contracts, the renewal of the teacher's contract or the termination of it after it has run its course, if done in accordance with the legal procedures established by the legislature, is a discretionary act of the board. Under the circumstances, as long as the school board has complied with the legal requirements pertaining to it, its discretion in the matter is not subject to court review. However, when the board employs a teacher and the law provides that a contract must be issued designating a specific period of time and a specific obligation of the board with respect to the contract, then a ministerial obligation clearly exists and the board can be compelled to perform in accordance with this responsibility.[5]

There is one other concept of considerable concern that governs the relationship of school board members to the structure of the schools. Authorities and court interpretations have almost universally held that in all matters in which the board is empowered to act, it must act as the total board. Individual members of the board, although they may perform ministerial duties for the board, may not act in behalf of the board. Certainly, in small school districts in which the school board retains a considerable amount of responsi-

---

[4] Hamilton and Reutter, *op. cit.*, p. 48.

[5] S. F. Roach, "School Boards and Teacher's Contract," *American School Journal*, 128 (March, 1954), 40–41.

bility for interviewing teachers and possibly even the selection of teachers, an individual school board member may act in behalf of the board in the interviewing of candidates, but he may not act in behalf of the board in the selection of a particular candidate. Individual school board members have been known to visit schools and request or demand that school employees do certain things. It is clearly outside the legal authority of any board member so to act, since in such matters the laws give the power to the board as a whole rather than to individual members of it.

Similarly, if the law specifically gives the power to act to the board as a whole, the board cannot delegate its authority to a single member thereof or to its executive officer. If the law requires the board to act, it must act as a whole at a legally constituted board meeting. Under most circumstances, outside of board meetings the school board member has no more legal authority over the operation of the school program than does any other individual citizen of the community.

From a legal point of view, school personnel do not interact with individual board members, but rather with the school board as a whole. Individual board members cannot perform their legal responsibilities through polling techniques or informal contacts outside the regularly designated and legally called school board meetings. A school employee who wishes to purchase a particular item does not have the authority to purchase the item when he obtains the permission of the individual board member independently. Such authority can only be given when the school board acts at a legally called school board meeting.

The Informal Roles of School Board Members

Laws prescribe the rules which govern the conduct of individuals in their relationships to one another. In another sense, laws prescribe the policies of the state with respect to the operations of specific functions that take place within it. Presumably, in a democracy the legal relationships of officials to employees of the government or to the public-at-large are governed by laws, as is indicated in the dictum that this is a government of law, not of men. But any person experienced in the affairs of government and of men knows that the human element cannot be eliminated from official actions or relationships. School board members are not mere creatures of the law who inevitably limit their actions to the bare necessities required by the law. Neither are the employees or patrons of the school district mere creatures of the law. The expectations and aspirations that individuals have for a particular relationship are of considerable consequence to the manner in which the relationship will be conducted. Under the circumstances, it is necessary to study the informal as well as the formal relationships of school board members in order to understand fully the manner in which school board members perform their responsibilities.

Unfortunately, there has been little detailed study of the informal relationships of school board members to other personnel in the school system. The research of Vidich and Bensman, Hollingshead, and Goldhammer, previously cited, indicates some of the essential aspects of these relationships. It does not, however, indicate all the mechanisms that operate in the informal government of the school. When individuals become members of the school board, they engage in their roles with a number of goals and perspectives which affect how they will conduct their official duties and how they will interact with members of the school staff.

School board members have a number of contacts outside official board meetings with both citizens of the community and employees of the school district, and in each of these contacts there is the potentiality that school business will be discussed, that school board members will become committed to particular points of view, and that action on particular school issues will be suggested and prescribed. If the human aspect of the relationship is not fully understood and controlled, it can lead to a considerable loss of effectiveness in the school board's operations.

Since the school board, by law, is delegated extensive power over the operations of the school organization, school board members are inevitably in some type of personal relationship with all the employees of the school district as well as with patrons who are particularly concerned or affected by the school program. This means that each school board member is in a visible position and can affect how other individuals involved in the school operation perform their respective roles. The relationship is more direct with some individuals than with others, and the position of school board members is more visible to them than to others.

The most frequent official contact of school board members in the performance of their duties is with the superintendent of schools and other members of the administrative staff. The superintendent acts as the executive officer of the board, and it is he who represents the rest of the organization to school board members. It is not unusual for the superintendent and school board members to have both personal and official contacts outside the regularly delegated school board meetings. The superintendent frequently contacts school board members in order to secure their points of view on problems which arise. Because of the level of income of the superintendent, he frequently engages in fraternal, social, and civic enterprises that are beyond the means of most of the members of the school staff, but which are also the types of activities which appear to be most attractive to school board members. It is not unusual for the school superintendent to have opportunities to visit informally to discuss school problems or other civic interests with individual members of his school board at fraternal organizations or civic luncheon clubs. It is not unusual, either, for the school board members in their endeavors to welcome the new administrator into the community to establish visiting patterns with him and, under the circumstances, to engage in many types of common social, recreational, and avocational enterprises.

In Holden's study of school board communication patterns in two different communities, only two of ten school board members reported any direct channels of communication with personnel in the school system. Of the ten school board members, six indicated that they had no frequent contacts with the superintendent outside regular school board meetings, but in each community the chairman of the board and one of the more influential board members reported that they maintained active communication channels with the superintendent. Holden concluded that active communication channels were maintained between those individuals who assumed leadership on the board, but only latent channels existed for those who were less aggressive.[6]

Goldhammer found that members of the school staff tended to look upon the superintendent as the school board's representative

---

[6] Louis Edward Holden, *Communication and Decision-Making in School Board-Superintendent Relations* (Unpublished Ed.D. dissertation, University of Oregon, 1961), pp. 103–6.

in the internal organization of the schools. This attitude developed as the result of their recognition of the fact that the superintendent was in the closest relationship to the members of the school board of any members of the staff, and that he shared with them many values which were designated as "managerial" values rather than the values of those who were the employees of the school organization. As a result of this informal relationship between the superintendent and the members of the school board, the teachers felt that there was a danger that their points of view would not be taken into consideration in school board deliberations. Both the formal and the informal structure of relationships within the school organization inevitably put the superintendent closer to the school board and caused him to express values within the organization that indicated his closer relationship to the points of view of the school board than of the members of the staff.[7]

Aside from their contact with the superintendent of schools, school board members also tend to have close relationships with other individuals within the community who look upon the school board members as their representatives in the school organization. Such individuals are likely to constitute a primary reference group for the school board member whose election to office and further acceptance in the community is based upon the degree to which he is an adequate representative of their points of view. Under the circumstances, when individuals come with specific problems to their friend who is on the school board, or who come with pleas for specific policies to be developed or for changes to be made, they are likely to find a very ready ear.

It is not unusual for a school board member to be in disagreement with what he considers to be the expectations of members of the community for the performance of his responsibilities or the expectations of the superintendent of schools or the members of the teaching staff. The school board member may frequently find himself in a position in which expectations for his performance are inconsistent, and no matter what action he takes he will offend some group to whom his conduct is visible and relevant.

The school board member is most visible and accessible to peo-

---

[7] Keith Goldhammer, *The Roles of School District Officials in Policy Determination in an Oregon Community* (Unpublished Ph.D. dissertation, University of Oregon, 1954), p. 230.

ple who are furthest removed from the primary relationship (the teacher-pupil relationship) over which he exerts authority and which will be directly affected by the decisions which he makes. He is least visible to those individuals who must carry out his policies and who constitute the main reason for the existence of the school. The law gives him authority to act in all matters; yet, the realities of the situation and the principles that have been developed through the experience of the educational profession restrict his getting direct information from teachers and pupils about how policies are actually carried out or what their effect may be upon the proper organization of the schools.

Except as they may be represented on special issues by their own representatives, teachers are represented before the board by administrators, and the board's image of the teacher is as conveyed by the administrator. School board members sometimes feel that their information is colored by the goals which the administrator has set to accomplish rather than by their being able to obtain an entirely true and objective appraisal of the situations with which they must deal.

Because teachers feel that they have been poorly represented, they have formed associations which endeavor to develop an image of the teaching profession more congenial to their point of view. Two such organizations are the teachers' associations, usually affiliated with the National Education Association, and the teachers' unions, the most prominent of which has been an affiliate of the American Federation of Labor. Both organizations, where they exist, generally have direct relationships with the school board, particularly on issues related to teacher welfare, tenure, and working conditions. School board members, under the circumstances, deal with the teachers as a group and, frequently, under conditions which have been established by perspectives outside the local situation. The local teachers may not always be entirely free to develop their own policies, since they are affected by the state and national policies developed by their organizations.

Aside from the formal remoteness of the school board members from the representatives of the teaching staff, there are occasions when school board members and teachers may get together. Teachers, too, belong to organizations within the community and often may constitute important clients or customers of school board members in their professional or business roles. School board members may forget about the necessity of maintaining the chain of command, and they may seek information directly from a teacher as they go about their normal professional or business routines. This may happen without the intention of violating either the principles of school board-staff relationships or the rules and regulations which the board has adopted.

The same may also be said for other employees of the school district. Although the board member is presumed to deal only with the school superintendent, and through him with the other members of the school staff, he may inevitably have some contacts with non-instructional employees of the school district in his normal community relationships. He will, undoubtedly, with or without the intention to secure first-hand information, discuss school problems with such personnel because these problems are an important part of the existence of both the school board member and the employee of the school district.

Inevitably the school board member is an outsider insofar as the internal operations of the schools are concerned. The law gives him authority over school operations, but the realities of the internal organization and the principles of effective organizational procedures necessitate that he remain aloof from the internal organization.

The essential problem for the school board in its relationship to the total organization is the fact that most of the information about how the schools operate and how personnel perform is second-hand information. It is given to the board for the purpose of creating in the minds of the members of the board the kind of image which the purveyor wants the board to have. It is unlikely that the situation can be otherwise. Since board members for the most part must earn their living and engage the major part of their time in personal pursuits, they cannot have intimate knowledge of the constant operations which take place within the schools. The guiding principles of school board-professional relationships are such that the school board member must attempt to refrain from seeking direct information from school employees and thereby destroying the chain of command within the school organization. Under the circumstances, school board members are constantly faced with the necessity of making decisions on the basis of imperfect and indirect knowledge of how those decisions will actually affect the proper education of the children within the school district.

The Emergence and Resolution of Conflict

There can be little doubt that the foregoing situation contains within it many potentialities for conflict both in superintendent-school board relationships and in teacher-school board relationships. It is also apparent that there is room for misunderstanding and resentment on the part of people in the community whose expectations for the performance of a school board member may be unrealistic in relation to the patterns of effective operation which must prevail.

Conflict in social situations arises when there are incongruous expectations for behavior on the part of different individuals, or when the behavior of individuals in social situations is outside the norms or standards set for them in those situations. School board members will not always find it compatible with their own expectations for their behavior to conform to either the policies established by their predecessors or the principles of school board relationships which arise out of the experience, research, and reflection of the educational profession. School board members may sometimes resent any limitations which are imposed upon their legal authority and may seek to exert their authority even at the expense of harmony within the schools.

There is no law that states that school board members must receive their information directly from the superintendent rather than from other employees of the school district. A board member may act entirely within the legal framework when he seeks to obtain first-hand information from teachers, janitors, or bus drivers about the effectiveness with which the superintendent is conducting his responsibilities. The fact that such behavior unquestionably undermines the authority of the superintendent and impairs his abilty to perform his responsibilities may not be important to the board member, but such behavior will almost inevitably lead to conflict, and may, as numerous instances reveal, produce disharmony within the school organization. Arbitrary or independent actions of individual school board members can produce serious consequences for the effectiveness of school operations.

How, then, can conflict be avoided while the school board still retains its legal authority, which by law it cannot delegate? The question is not easy to answer; neither is there any specific research which can be cited to provide a definitive answer. Research and theory with respect to group relations, however, suggest at least two procedures which are worthy of consideration.

First, conflict can generally be avoided by establishing honest and cooperative relationships with subordinate personnel. School employees are remote from school board meetings, and they sometimes suspect that school board members and administrators express attitudes which are inimicable to their interests. When a school board member is quoted as making hostile remarks about personnel, their fears appear to be verified. Thorough understanding of the problems of employees is needed by school board members, and caution must be exercised to assure personnel that board members are not irrevocably hostile to their interests. Some school boards make it a point to have representatives of various categories of employees present at board meetings, and they endeavor to meet with groups to reduce the social distance that exists between the employees and the board members. This also reduces the degree to which the school board must act on exclusively second-hand information.

Second, clearly stated policies which define the roles of participants in an organization are necessary so that individuals can clearly understand their official obligations as well as those of others associated with them. These policies should be written, and they should be subject to constant review, evaluation, and revision. School board members should not have to accept a given statement because it was adopted by their predecessors, but there should be agreement among board members and administrators that all concerned will accept the policy statements to which the majority has agreed. A written statement of policies establishes the foundation for securing mutual expectations for the performance of responsibilities. It also establishes, at least informally, the rules and boundaries for acceptable action.

Above all, experience shows that school board members, administrators, teachers, and other school employees must seek to develop a team spirit in which each participant recognizes the contributions being made by other participants and the mutuality of interests involved. Differences in the social structure are inevitable, and various participants will have different roles to perform in order to help make the organization work. Recognizing that problems exist, however, the team member will promote harmony to the extent that he recognizes a need for compromise when potential conflict arises.

CHAPTER V

How School Boards Conduct Their Business: The Decision-Making Process

The Function of the School Board Meeting

The school board meeting is the legally designated instrument through which the school board transacts its business. The official handbook of the California School Boards Association states that California law permits school boards to act only at officially designated meetings.[1] Unlike membership on regulatory or administrative boards, school board membership involves a team effort on the part of the participants, and no school board member has any authority to act alone. Each school board member has an official capacity in relation to the schools only at school board meetings.

The basic function of the school board meeting is the transaction of the business of the school board. Any business of the school district which requires board action must come before the board at legal meetings. Neither the school district nor the school board are committed to any decisions or policies except when action has been taken and recorded in the minutes of the board meeting. Although school boards may meet as a committee of the whole, divide themselves into operating committees, or meet informally with school officials or school patrons, no action of any part of the board, or of the board as a whole, is legal unless transacted in a meeting as prescribed by law.

Characteristics of School Board Meetings

There are certain characteristics of state laws governing school board meetings. State laws generally designate that school boards must hold regular meetings. Sometimes the frequency of such meet-

---

[1] James, ed., *op. cit.*, p. 11.

ings, such as once a month, is designated. The laws generally indicate that the school board must meet at a regularly designated place, such as a school building in the district. The laws also generally indicate that every meeting must be open to the public, although in some instances executive sessions are expressly permitted for specific purposes, such as the determination of matters pertaining to personnel or discussions affecting financial transactions which, if prematurely publicized, would impair the economy of the school district. The National Education Association reported in 1946 that 60 per cent of the school boards reporting held meetings which were open to the public, although school board meetings were generally very poorly attended.[2] As late as 1955, however, two researchers found that in Texas only a few more than half the school board members and school administrators believed school board meetings should be open to the public.[3] Favorable attitudes toward public attendance were expressed more by large city boards than by small town and rural school boards.

Generally, there are three types of school board meetings at which business may be transacted: regular, adjourned, and special. A *regular meeting* is one held in accordance with a prearranged schedule at which school board business is normally transacted. School boards generally hold at least one regular meeting a month, but in the larger school districts it is characteristic for not less than two regular monthly meetings to be held. Frequently, in the larger school districts, the school board holds a meeting of the committee-of-the-whole prior to a regular meeting. The committee-of-the-whole meetings are open to the public unless personnel matters or delicate financial transactions are under consideration. These meetings afford an opportunity for board members to ask detailed questions about specific problems, thus enabling aspects of the school board's business to be transacted at the regular meeting with dispatch so that the board can concentrate upon those aspects of its agenda which are of greatest concern.

There is no limitation upon the nature of the business that can come before the board at a regular meeting. Generally, the board

2 National Education Association, *Status and Practices of Boards of Education,* Research Bulletin, Vol. XXIV, No. 2 (Washington, D.C.: The Association, 1946).
3 Bascom B. Hayes and Donald G. Nugent, *How Do School Boards Function?* (Austin: Texas Association of School Boards, 1955).

is permitted by law to establish its own rules, regulations, and policies relative to the conduct of school board meetings. It is most common for a school board to consider matters which are brought to its attention by the superintendent of schools in the form of the meeting agenda or to listen to any particular petitions or requests that are made by patrons of the school district through the superintendent of schools.

An *adjourned meeting* is one which is usually held as a continuation of a regular or a special meeting. Sometimes, when school boards discuss delicate or difficult problems, it is impossible for a decision to be made or the entire agenda for the meeting to be completed. Under the circumstances, it is possible for the school board to adjourn the meeting to a subsequent day or time and continue the regular meeting.

Special meetings are meetings which are called for a particular purpose at an irregular time. State laws do not generally designate whether special meetings must be held at a regular meeting place of the board, although authorities recognize that all school board meetings, whether special or regular, should be held at a regularly designated meeting place, which should be readily accessible to the public. The laws generally recognize that there must be a notice given by the proper school board officials for the calling of a special meeting, and the call for the special meeting must specifically state the nature of the business that is to be transacted. Legally, no business may be transacted at a special meeting that is not specifically indicated in the call.

Because school boards are given broad latitude by state laws with respect to the conduct of meetings, practices vary to a considerable extent. There are some practices, however, that are generally recognized as desirable and are usually followed by boards. It is generally recognized by authorities, for instance, that a school board meeting should be held in accordance with a predetermined agenda. The agenda should be developed by the superintendent of schools, and a tentative draft of the agenda should be sent in advance of the meeting to all board members, the press and other interested communication media, subordinate administrative officers, officers of educational organizations, and interested citizens of the community. School board members should be encouraged to suggest additional items that might be incorporated on the agenda in advance of school board meetings. However, a sufficient time prior to the meeting must be given to the superintendent so that he can prepare materials for his recommendations on items which members of the board wish to add to the agenda. It is usually recognized by authorities that school boards should not act upon any matter brought to a school board's attention at the board meeting until such time as the administrative staff has had a complete opportunity to study it thoroughly.

It is recognized as a desirable practice for the administrator to distribute to the members of the school board an information brochure in which the background information required by board members is presented. Such information brochures are generally distributed several days prior to a school board meeting. They contain information in support of each of the items on the agenda and also the superintendent's recommendations and the reasons in support thereof. Some superintendents list the alternatives which the board should consider and the potential consequences of each.

The law requires that an official set of minutes be kept to record all the transactions of the school district. In no case does the law specify the detail with which the minutes must be kept, and practices vary to a considerable extent. Minutes are generally poorly kept, and particularly in the smaller school districts, record nothing except the official action of the board. These minimal board minutes actually meet the requirements of the law, but it is questionable whether they fully meet the needs of the school organization for recording the discussions of the board members and some of the informal transactions which occur at meetings. Authorities in educational administration are generally agreed that the minutes should be extensive and should record the information that adequately describes the total setting of the board meeting and the gist of the discussions that take place. In this fashion the school administrators, as well as the public and board members, can use the minutes for information purposes in determining the manner in which policies of the board can be interpreted. Minutes must be kept in an official book, and in most states they are a public document that can be reviewed by interested citizens upon request.

The length and the setting of board meetings are considered critical concerns by authorities, but practices vary to a considerable extent. A Study by R. H. Brown of school board members in cities of 5,000 to 300,000 population showed that time spent in meetings has greatly increased. In 1926, board members spent, on the average, 51 hours in school board meetings annually; but in 1952, they reported spending 88 hours annually in board meetings.[4]

It is not uncommon for some boards to begin their meetings shortly after dinner and to continue until the early hours of the morning. A few boards, particularly in large cities, have daytime meetings, generally in the late afternoon. Some authorities disagree with this practice on the basis that it prevents people who are employed from participating. It should be recognized, however, that changing cultural conditions now require that an increasing percentage of the population be employed during the evening hours, and, at any time the board meets, some individuals may be denied access as a result of conflict with their working hours.

Other boards, however, may rigidly limit the length of the meeting, attempting to conduct the school district's business in two or three hours. The knowledge gained from research in the dynamics of decision-making groups indicates that a school board probably becomes less efficient and increasingly less able to make decisions as the meeting is prolonged. Few, if any, meetings should last more than three hours, and it is undoubtedly true that the efficiency of the group tends to decrease after two hours of meeting time.

The practices of school boards also vary to a considerable extent with respect to the place and setting of the meeting. Larger school districts tend to have a formally arranged school board room in which the members sit at a large table or podium in the front of the room. Administrators may sit with the members or at a table in front of the board for the presentation of their reports. The press usually sits at a separate table in front of the board. It is not uncommon in smaller school districts for the board to sit around a table in the principal's office or in the school library, with relatively little space allocated for spectators and no particular arrangements made for the press other than that generally allocated for the audience. Many authorities consider it unwise for the setting of the board to be too informal, since the board is conducting the public's business which involves concern for the children of the community and the expenditure of large amounts of money.

---

[4] R. H. Brown, "Composition of School Boards," *American School Board Journal*, 129 (August, 1954), 23–24.

One of the important issues affecting the operation of school boards is whether or not school boards should employ standing committees. Standing committees usually are responsible for certain administrative actions, and since most authorities believe that the board's attention should be directed to the development of policy, leaving administrative concerns to the superintendent, they believe standing committees interfere with the proper role of the school board and create friction between the superintendent and the members of the school board. Deffenbaugh reported in 1927 that most large city school boards conducted their business through standing committees, such as committees on personnel, transportation, purchasing, operation and maintenance, curriculum, and so forth.[5] In a 1946 study, the National Education Association reported that 53 per cent of the city school districts had no standing committees on their boards, while 88 per cent of the noncity school districts lacked standing committees.[6] Stapley studied the attitudes of school boards in Indiana and found that most of them felt that standing committees were undesirable.[7] Rice sampled a cross section of superintendents throughout the United States. He discovered that those who work with standing committees of school boards generally like them, while those who do not work with such committees look with disfavor upon them. Approximately 75 per cent of the school administrators preferred to work with a school board which met as a committee-of-the-whole.[8] The evidence shows that standing committees are increasingly being discarded in favor of committee-of-the-whole meetings and the delegation of administrative responsibilities to the superintendent of schools.

It is a fairly common practice for school boards to have executive sessions prior to regular meetings in order to discuss critical problems and to come to some agreements prior to the open board meeting. Sometimes the press is admitted to such meetings but

---

[5] W. Deffenbaugh, *Certain Practices in City School Administration*, U.S. Bureau of Education, City School Leaflet, No. 29 (Washington, D.C.: Government Printing Office, 1927).

[6] National Education Association, *Status and Practices of Boards of Education*, p. 63.

[7] Maurice E. Stapley, "Attitudes and Opinions of School Board Members in Indiana's Cities and Towns," *Indiana University School of Education Bulletin*, No. 27 (March, 1951).

[8] Arthur W. Rice, "Most Superintendents Reject Standing Committees of The School Board," *The Nation's School*, Vol. 55 (January, 1955), 65.

pledged to treat the information as privileged until such time as it is officially released. Such meetings are expressly prohibited in California under the provisions of the Brown Act, which specifically designates the only conditions under which executive sessions of public bodies can be held. The objection to such sessions rests upon the contention that the board is transacting the public's business and that the public has a right to know not only the actions taken by the board, but also the full discussion and rationale for the action and the roles played in the decision process by all the participants. Such sessions are defended on the premise that the public's best interests are sometimes ill-served by the premature publicity that is given. It is also necessary for the board and administration to protect the interests of children and employees when personnel matters are under discussion. It is also contended that an administrator needs occasions when he can have frank, informal, and confidential discussions with his board. The central issue is actually less one of the propriety of such sessions than of the safeguards established to protect the public's interest and the discretion employed.

What School Boards Do at Meetings

Authorities on school administration generally agree that the major function of the school board is the determination of policies. Cunningham suggests that this is a loosely defined term which in actual practice means relatively little. Goldhammer made a detailed study of the substance of school board meetings in a small community over a period of one year and found that members felt that they should spend more time on curriculum matters. Actually, they spent very little of their time on items on which they were most inclined to express concern. Goldhammer found that most of their time was devoted to routine housekeeping and managerial chores required of them by law and which did not involve what Cunningham describes as the policy-making function. The board spent 30 per cent of the total time at school board meetings during the year on personnel matters, 30 per cent on what Goldhammer termed "nonprogrammatic" details, 24 per cent on business and finance, and only 16 per cent on programmatic details. He noted that the members were sometimes critical of the time that they consumed on minor and technical details, but that they were never able to work out an approach so that routine could be handled simply and expeditiously.[9]

Cunningham describes three types of decisions that school boards make: (1) housekeeping decisions, which involved the acceptance of reports, formal acknowledgment of reports and correspondence, votes of appreciation, and the determination of procedures; (2) administrative (terminal action) decisions, which involved the purchasing of school sites, adding to insurance coverage, the borrowing of funds, granting exclusions to the compulsory school attendance law, and calling for bids on bonds (these were decisions which the boards were legally required to make, and for which they could not shift the responsibility to some other employee); and (3) policy decisions, which served as guidelines to administrative action and which existed as a rule or a law exists in other social contacts. Cunningham further noted that out of 187 decisions which a school board made during an eight-month period, 61 (or 33 per cent) were housekeeping decisions; 110 (or 59 per cent) were administrative decisions; and 16 (or 8 per cent) were policy decisions.[10]

Experience in working with boards indicates that they spend a considerable amount of their time working on technical details involving primarily the managerial aspects of school operations; they leave the major policy decisions concerning the educational program to the professional staff.

Patterns of Conducting
School Board Meetings

Although there are many attempts to develop typologies for the description of the patterns of conducting school board meetings, there appear to be three general classifications into which most meetings fall. These may be described as (1) the formal pattern, (2) the town-forum pattern, and (3) the discussion-group pattern.

The formal pattern. The formal pattern is based upon a rigid model of parliamentary procedure. In this pattern a written agenda is prepared. The chairman dominates the meeting and calls upon

[9] Goldhammer, *The Roles of School District Officials in Policy-Determination in an Oregon Community,* p. 205.

[10] Luvern L. Cunningham, "Decision-Making Behavior of School Boards," *American School Board Journal,* 144 (February, 1962), 13–16.

the various members who address the chair. All action is taken by formal vote of the members, and a consistent routine is followed by limiting discussion to items that are brought before the board through the motions of the members or through the presentation of reports by members of the administrative staff, particularly the superintendent. In relatively few instances, even among large school districts, has the pattern been found to be as rigid as that of city councils, which make their decisions primarily through the enactment of ordinances. Even in the formal pattern, decisions are generally made by simple motions, and only when the laws require formal presentation of resolutions are decisions made in such a fashion. Parliamentary procedure is generally followed, however, and the attempt is made to conduct the business of the board in a legalistic frame of reference. Participation of the audience is limited by the policies of the board, and each action of the board, when recorded in the minutes, is carefully codified so that any decision can be readily identified as a part of the general policy of the school district. The formal pattern prevails to the greatest extent among large city school boards and to the least extent among the small rural school boards.

The town-forum pattern. The town-forum pattern is more informal, and school board members are joined by citizens in an informal situation in which anyone who wishes to speak is given the opportunity to do so on any issue that arises. Generally, the audience is separated from the board in its seating arrangement. The endeavor is made to reach a consensus prior to the time that a vote is taken, and a measure that involves any considerable amount of opposition is discussed for a lengthy period in order to attempt to reconcile opposing factions. This pattern involves the participation of individuals who are not on the board and who are not legally accorded the authority for making decisions affecting the school district. Boards following this style, however, proceed on the premise that the greater amount of the participation of the community in the affairs of the school district, the lesser will be the danger of conflict with respect to school problems.

Formal action of the board is generally taken by the motion of members. Boards which use this pattern of conducting their business usually are sensitive to the wishes of the community and frequently delay action in order to provide opportunity for either board members or the administrative staff to consult with citizens of the community on particularly controversial issues. This pattern of operation is frequently found in all sizes of school districts.

The discussion-group pattern.   In the experience of the writer, the most frequent pattern of operation of school boards is the discussion-group type. School boards tend to be informal in the manner in which they conduct their business. Most school board meetings take place around a conference table, and the audience, if any, is generally asked to sit at the table with the board and to participate in the informal discussions. Usually, issues are discussed until there is a feeling that a consensus has been established; only then is a motion made to record the action.

Both Cunningham and Goldhammer found that there was a tendency to avoid the actual taking of a vote. Cunningham points out that even on important issues some decisions of school boards are made merely by head nodding, as the chairman assumes that a consensus has been reached. In contrasting the formal and the informal approaches, Cunningham indicates that the chairman of the board largely determines the patterns of decision making which will prevail on the board. He says that if the chairman is determined "to go by the book," the registering of group decision is likely to be formal. If, however, the chairman is more permissive in his perspective, he is likely to accept a consensus of the group as its official action. Cunningham noted that groups operating under controversy tend to be formal, while those groups that operate in a more favorable situation tend to be less formal.

Cunningham also noted that very few split votes arose as a result of the discussion method. A considerable amount of time was spent on discussion, and the board chairman generally delayed taking the vote or determining the consensus until he was fairly sure that unanimity prevailed. Cunningham also attempted to determine whether or not there were any differences in the manner of conducting business on different types of decisions that had to be made. He found, however, that the percentage of policy decisions made through consensus was as high as that for either administrative or housekeeping decisions.[11]

---

11 *Ibid.*

How Decisions Are Reached

Unquestionably, each board has its own methods of operation. The two key figures in a school board are the chairman of the school board and the superintendent of schools. The chairman of the board is a key person because it is he who is responsible for conducting the meeting and for assisting the board in accomplishing the transaction of the business that is before it. To the extent that he is a weak leader of a formal group, the board is very likely to flounder; individual board members may vie for the position of informal leadership; and the process of policy determination may become erratic and confused. To the extent that he is a forceful leader of the group, it is likely that the board will become highly goal-directed and will transact its business with efficiency. Democratic procedures, however, may be restricted.

The superintendent is a key member of the school board because he possesses information that is vital to the board in the proper transaction of its affairs. To the extent that he is capable of relating this information directly and effectively to the board, he can materially improve the efficiency with which the board determines its policies and accomplishes its work.

Both Cunningham and Goldhammer, working in different communities with prolonged studies of school boards, identified five stages in the decision-making process. Cunningham's five stages are as follows:

1. *The initiation of the policy-making process.* The policy-making process begins at a point when a problem has been raised before the group. The person who identifies these problems may be a school board member, an administrator, some person in the school organization on a subordinate level, or even some outsider to the school organization or the policy-making group. The need for action is communicated to the school board through a variety of means: formally, through the press or other communication media; informally, through the contacts of citizens of the community with members of the school board and superintendent; or directly, through administrators at constituted board meetings.

2. *The definition and statement of the policy problem.* One of the first problems of the policy-making group is to obtain a common orientation to the problem which it confronts. This is common

not only of the school board but also of all decision-making groups. One of the most significant problems in this respect that Cunningham isolated was the degree to which members attempted to define the problem confronting it in terms of their personal goals and value preferences. A considerable period of time had to be spent in defining the problem so that a common orientation could be obtained before the issues involved could be resolved.

3. *Deliberation, bargaining, gathering and weighing of information, and raising and assaying alternates.* Cunningham noted that this stage involved a considerable amount of maneuvering for position by school board members as attempts were made to redefine the problem. Individual members attempted to obtain definitions which would enable them to secure action which accorded with their values. Cunningham also noted that it was in this stage of the policy-making process that coalitions of members were formed on controversial issues, and that the board, when unanimity did not exist, was actually divided into subgroups. Bargaining took place between groups in the endeavor to reach a workable conclusion.

4. *Policy enactment.* After bargaining and the transaction between subgroups have taken place, it is possible for the board to develop a policy and to make a statement of its position which can be used as a guide to the superintendent for conducting the affairs of the school district.

5. *The consequences of policy action—testing and evaluation.* Following the enactment of policy, a period ensues in which the school board and the administrators attempt to evaluate the consequences of their decision for the operation of the school organization.[12]

Goldhammer's identification of five stages of the decision process, based both upon an interaction analysis and an interpretation of the substantive content of the school board meetings, involved the following:

1. The superintendent or some other board member introduced a problem to the members of the board.

2. The superintendent presented a brief statement on the background of the problem and the issues involved, and then made his recommendation to the board.

---

[12] Luvern L. Cunningham, *A Community Develops Educational Policy* (Unpublished Ed.D. dissertation, University of Oregon, 1958), pp. 398–422.

3. The members questioned the superintendent for further information and the analysis of the data that he had given to them.

4. The members raised questions about the recommendation, introduced issues related to the main topic under consideration, introduced alternative proposals, and either agreed upon the recommendation or worked out new ones. Usually some regularization of the information in hand was sought so that justification for the final proposal arose out of the discussion.

5. Three alternatives were then used. The first involved making a motion, which was seconded and carried, and was followed by the calling for the next order of business. The second alternative involved the chairman's inquiry relative to whether or not a motion was necessary. He usually declared, at the same time, that it was his opinion that consensus had already been reached, no motion was necessary, and the clerk could proceed to record the action without cluttering up the books with motions. The matter was then usually dropped. The third alternative involved a statement that the information was not sufficient for the members to come to a conclusion, so the matter was deferred for further study and investigation. The superintendent usually was asked to furnish specific information on the topic at the next board meeting.[13]

Various researchers have shown the critical relationship of the superintendent of schools to the school board in the structuring of the deliberative process. In Goldhammer's study, 72 per cent of the interaction at board meetings took place between the superintendent and members of the school board, with only 28 per cent of the interaction taking place among the members themselves without reference to the superintendent. This was probably a more extreme pattern than generally exists, since the chairman of the board was highly directive and engaged the superintendent in careful cross-examination on every issue that arose. Thirty-two per cent of the interaction that took place at the board meetings was the interchange between the superintendent and the chairman of the board. However, with a more permissive chairman and a superintendent who relied more heavily on written documentation of his recommendations, a more general distribution of participation among all the members of the board would probably prevail.

---

[13] Goldhammer, *The Roles of School District Officials in Policy-Determination in an Oregon Community*, pp. 190–92.

Because the superintendent gave little written information to the board, the dominant role played by school board members in the deliberative process was that of seeking information, while the dominant role of the superintendent of schools was that of giving information.[14]

Shock found a somewhat different pattern in his study of a California school board. The superintendent relied more heavily on written materials and attempted to play a less overt role in the deliberative process. Eighty-six per cent of the decisions recorded involved the acceptance of the recommendations of the superintendent. Shock found that the superintendent's recommendations were accepted in most instances on matters that could be considered professional, while there was more inclination to suggest alternatives to the superintendent's recommendations on matters of finance. Since the chairman and the superintendent of the board displayed personality characteristics different from those in Goldhammer's study, more emphasis was placed upon the analysis and interpretation of data than upon the actual seeking of information.[15]

Influences Affecting the School Board in the Making of Decisions

As indicated in Chapter II, many influences impinge upon the school board in making of decisions. Holden showed that there was considerable communication between school board members and citizens of the community as well as representatives of the school organization. He noted that this communication took place both within and outside school board meetings, and that there was evidence in the decisions made by the school boards in both communities that board members were affected by the pressures put upon them by citizens in the community.[16]

Mattlin discovered that on twelve issues studied in detail and upon which school boards in Nassau and Suffolk counties in New York had to act, considerable pressure was exerted by community

---

[14] *Ibid.*, p. 183.

[15] Donald Paul Shock, *Patterns in the Decision-Making Process of a School Board* (Unpublished Ed.D. dissertation, Stanford University, 1960).

[16] Louis Edward Holden, *Communication and Decision-Making in School Board-Superintendent Relations* (Unpublished Ed.D. dissertation, University of Oregon, 1961).

groups; but ten of the issues in particular were chronic causes for pressure. He concluded that school boards cannot reflect the thinking of the majority of the citizens of the school district because their policy decisions are frequently determined by the political necessity to appease articulate minority groups. In rapidly growing communities, pressures were related primarily to the provision of school facilities and school finances. Although members appeared equally responsive to pressures on all issues, the responsiveness was greater for issues that were chronic causes for pressure.[17]

Tucker's study of school board decision making in South Carolina showed that community connections of board members which were personal, fraternal, social, professional, business, and so forth, formed pressures that had a definite bearing on how individual board members made their decisions. The evidence showed that some board members tended to ignore much of this influence, while others were considerably swayed by it. Tucker concluded that there was more of an inclination of a school board to yield to pressures when it made its decisions on the basis of current issues than was true when a board made some long-range plans and adopted appropriate long-range policies as guides to future administrative actions. He was also of the opinion that some boards tended to act primarily in response to pressure as the result of their failure to adopt long-range policies.[18]

On the basis of the evidence, it is apparent that board members attempt to consider the perspectives of individuals in the community as well as their contacts with people in the school organization. There is evidence also to suggest that school board members are affected by the pressures and experiences of their own families. Information secured by a wife at a bridge club, by a husband at Rotary, or by children at the dinner table may be used at the next board meeting as the basis for making certain important decisions affecting the schools.

Since board members are human, one cannot expect them to be indifferent to the pressures which normally are imposed upon individuals when they occupy official positions in the community. The

---

[17] Howard Barry Mattlin, *Community Pressures on School Board Members in Nassau and Suffolk Counties, New York* (Unpublished Ed.D. dissertation, New York University, 1960).

[18] Cecil I. Tucker, "The School Board's Decisions," *The University of South Carolina Education Report,* Vol. V, No. 4 (April, 1962).

informality with which most school boards conduct their business is a further incentive to permit irrelevant information and uninformed pressures to guide or even determine the outcomes of the board's actions. The solution to the improvement of the board's decision making appears to lie in the improvement of the deliberative process. Board members need to study the actual process which they employ in order to determine the extent to which they make decision making an empirical search for general principles rather than a loose discussion group basing its important decisions on evidence which may not meet the criteria of acceptability. Decisions made by the school board are of vital concern not only to the various interest groups in the community but also to such outside groups whose programs or business are affected by the decisions a local board makes. It is not uncommon for overt and subtle pressures to be directed upon school boards from diverse elements. Unfortunately, there is no research on this issue to assist in developing a full perspective of how these influences operate.

CHAPTER VI

The School Board Member

Why Individuals Become
School Board Members

In 1927, when George S. Counts wrote his pioneering work, *The Social Composition of Boards of Education,* he ably stated a principle which has become axiomatic for writers in school administration. He indicated that the degree to which the school could fulfill its social responsibilities was dependent upon "the good will, the courage, and the intelligence" of school board members. He added that "the qualitative advance of public education must depend as much on the decisions of the board of education as on the development of the science and philosophy of education."[1] There are few, if any, who have had close association with school boards who would disagree with this statement. Since Counts' study there has been growing awareness of the importance of school board membership in achieving adequate educational programs, but very little has been done to explore the motivations citizens have to become school board members.

Important as school membership is, on the whole it appears to be a critical position fraught with many dangers and one in which the incumbent almost always sits on the edge of conflict. Experience shows that many school board members have suffered personal injuries and have had to expend large amounts of their own money in order to render to the community a service for which they receive no remuneration and little recognition. Indeed, one must conclude that the personal satisfactions must be extremely great for individuals to want to serve in this position.

Garmire made a study in the Willamette Valley of Oregon on the

---

[1] George S. Counts, *The Social Composition of Boards of Education* (Chicago: The University of Chicago Press, 1927), p. 1.

reasons individuals gave for wanting to become members of school boards. His findings are presented in Table 1. They show that

TABLE 1

REASONS FOR SEEKING OFFICE

Reasons	Percentage
1. General interest in education	37.6
2. Civic duty or community service interest	33.0
3. Influenced by friends, relatives, or acquaintances	33.0
4. Children in school and a desire to see that they had a good education	24.0
5. Felt the capacity to serve	15.6
6. To represent a group in the community	10.1
7. Opposed a school board policy	9.2
8. For self-satisfaction	7.3
9. Interested in seeing that the taxes were properly administered	7.3
10. Opposed to a school board member	6.4
11. Appointed	6.4
12. Ran because of the reorganization issue in the district	3.7

Source: Leonard Garmire, "A Study of the Attitudes of School Board Members as They Relate to the Reasons for Seeking Office," *Oregon School Study Council Bulletin,* Vol. 6, No. 2 (Eugene, Oregon: The School of Education, University of Oregon, 1962), 7.

reasons for seeking office are divided into three categories. Garmire has identified these categories as self-interest, service interest, and neutral.

The self-interest category involves such items as "children in school and a desire to see that they had a good education," "opposed a school board policy," "for self-satisfaction," and "opposed to a school board member." The service-interest group involves altruistic reasons for seeking office and either an interest in serving the interests of the community or of promoting the welfare of the educational function. Some individuals were neutral and became members because they were asked to do so, while for other individuals it was apparent that motivations were a mixture of both self-interest and service-interest items.

The evidence collected by Garmire shows that more than a third of the members listed such items as a general interest in education, a civic duty or community service interest, or the influence of friends, relatives, or acquaintances. Garmire's analysis showed that 33 per cent of the responses of school board members indicated a service interest; 29.4 per cent showed both service interest and self-interest; 26.6 per cent showed only a self-interest; and 11 per cent were classified as neutral.

Garmire found that the general school board population did not consider that educational or community issues played an important part in their decisions to seek office. Three-fourths of the new school board members, however, indicated that issues were important in their decisions to seek office. Garmire concluded that this phenomenon was undoubtedly due to either the fact that the proximity of the election made the recall of new members more accurate or that experienced school board members had become involved in the issues and problems which arose after their election and that the original issues had become obscured or resolved.[2]

There were some interesting relationships between certain demographic variables and the expression of service interest on the school board. In general, it could be stated that the higher the level of educational attainment, the greater was the percentage of response of service interest. Those with no religious identifications gave a higher percentage of response on self-interest items. Protestant identifications were higher on service-interest identification than those of Catholics, whose responses were a greater mixture of service-interest and self-interest identifications due to their expressed need for denominational representation on local school boards. Women board members expressed a higher service interest than men; and in the occupational groups, farmers, skilled workers, and machine operators more often gave self-interest reasons for seeking board membership than any other occupational groups.

There appear to be two primary types of motivation for seeking school board membership. First, individuals become members of the school board because they want to render an important service to the community or to youth. Second, members are motivated as the result of their being dissatisfied with some person or policy. It is certainly apparent that the combination of motives probably helps each candidate make his decision. Goldhammer's findings (see Chapter II) also indicate that the idealism of board members in seeking membership as the result of the desire to render some

---

[2] Leonard Garmire, "A Study of the Attitudes of School Board Members As They Relate to the Reasons for Seeking Office," *Oregon School Study Council Bulletin,* Vol. 6, No. 2 (Eugene, Oregon: School of Education, University of Oregon, 1962), 15.

service is also related to certain values which they hold and wish to see perpetuated through public education. Relatively few board members, however, appear to sustain entirely self-interest motives after they gain experience on the board. Most individuals seem to accept school board membership as a primary reference group, and most seem to promote the interests of public education, to which they have developed an intense commitment.

The Social Status of School Board Members

The first intensive study of the social composition of school boards was made by Counts in 1927. Counts, however, cites in his study three previous studies whose findings are approximately the same. One was by Scott Nearing in 1916. His study showed that there was a concentration of board members' occupations in a relatively small number of categories. His data indicated that 144 of the 967 board members studied were merchants; 78 were manufacturers; and 104 were bankers, brokers, real estate men, and insurance men; 333 professional men were included on boards, and of them one-third (or 118) were doctors and dentists, and two-fifths (or 144) were lawyers. Of the board members included in the study, 588 (or 61 per cent) came from the occupational classifications of merchants, manufacturers, bankers, brokers, real estate men, doctors, and lawyers.[3]

In 1919 the teachers' union of New York City also made a study which covered 67 cities with populations of more than 40,000. In only 17 of these cities were representatives of labor included on the board.[4]

In 1922 Struble made a study of 169 cities with populations of more than 2,500 and less than 250,000 inhabitants. Of the 761 men on the school boards, only 54 were classed as manual laborers. Approximately 60 per cent of the members were drawn from five occupational groups, including merchants, bankers, lawyers, physicians, and business executives.[5]

---

[3] Scott Nearing, "Who's Who on Our School Boards," School and Society, 5 (January 20, 1907), 5; quoted in Counts, op. cit., 3.

[4] "Few Cities Have Labor on Board of Education," The Headgear Worker, 4 (November 21, 1919), 3; quoted in Counts, op. cit., 4.

[5] George G. Struble, "A Study of School Board Personnel," American School Board Journal, 65 (October, 1922), 48–49, 137–38; quoted in Counts, op. cit., 4.

The findings of Counts' study coincided with the previous ones that had been made. In the rural areas, 95 per cent of the male members of public school boards were involved in agricultural activities; but on city boards, 32 per cent were proprietors; 30 per cent were professionals; and 14 per cent came from managerial occupations. Only 8 per cent were involved in manual labor.[6]

Counts' findings have been roughly duplicated by several more recent studies. A study by the National Education Association in 1946 showed that of all boards 28 per cent of the members were proprietors and executives; 27 per cent were farmers; 15 per cent were professionals; 7 per cent were housewives; and all other occupational categories had 6 or less per cent each of the total. Rural and small town school boards were dominated by farmers, while city school boards had higher percentages of proprietors, executives, and professionals.[7]

Hunter made a study of the social composition of Louisiana Parish school boards in 1949 and discovered that most of them came from select economic groups in the community and enjoyed success in their economic endeavors.[8]

Hines studied the Eugene, Oregon, school board from the period of 1891 to 1944 and concluded that the board at all times represented the business and professional community. During this 53-year period, there were a total of 60 men and women on the board. Thirty-three were in business; 19 were in the professions; and 8 were housewives. The working class and farm groups were never directly represented.[9]

Brown's study in 1953 of the composition of school boards in cities of 5,000 to 300,000 population showed that 69.3 per cent of the board members were proprietors, managers, or professionals.[10]

In 1958, Albert studied 396 school boards in cities of over 30,000. His replies represented 2,688 board members from all 48 states. He compared the composition of school boards in 1945 and 1958 and found that professionals, proprietors, and executives were

[6] Counts, *op. cit.*, p. 52.
[7] National Education Association, *op. cit.*, p. 53.
[8] J. A. Hunter, "Social Composition of Louisiana Parish School Boards," *American School Board Journal*, 119 (October and November, 1949), 17–19.
[9] Hines, *op. cit.*
[10] Brown, "The Composition of School Boards."

the occupational groups most frequently represented in both years.[11]

Both Holden's and Goldhammer's studies came to the same conclusions. Holden reported that in Riverside all board members represented business interests and had considerable communication with the business and professional elements of the community.[12] Goldhammer showed that board members were known as men of economic substance in the community and that they represented primarily the interests of the proprietary group in the community.[13]

Tiedt did a companion study to Garmire's on characteristics of school board members in the Willamette Valley in Oregon, and he discovered that 61 per cent of the board members came from professional, managerial, and technical occupations in their communities.[14] He concluded that school board members are not representative of the general population since they tend to come from social and economic groups which have higher incomes, a higher level of economic and educational attainment, and more prestige in the community.[15] He substantiates his findings by making comparisons of the average characteristics of the school board members of the Willamette Valley with the averages for the 1960 census of population in Oregon. He found that 63 per cent of the school board members had some college education, while the average educational attainment of the population in Oregon was grade 10.9. Sixty-one per cent of the school board members came from professional, managerial, and technical operations, while the national average (data were not available for Oregon) was 24 per cent. The average income of the Oregon school board members was $9,000, while the average income of the adult population in Oregon was $6,600. Ninety-one per cent of the school board members were male, while 49 per cent of the Oregon population were male; and 99 per cent of the school board members were married, while only

[11] Frank Robert Albert, Jr., *Selected Characteristics of School Board Members and Their Attitudes Towards Certain Criticism of Public School Education* (Unpublished Ph.D. dissertation, University of Mississippi, 1959).

[12] Holden, *op. cit.,* p. 132.

[13] Keith Goldhammer, "Community Power Structure and School Board Membership," *American School Board Journal,* 130 (March, 1955), 23–25.

[14] Sidney W. Tiedt, "Oregon School Board Members in the Willamette Valley," *Oregon School Study Council Bulletin,* Vol. 6, No. 6 (Eugene, Oregon: School of Education, University of Oregon, 1962), 7.

[15] *Ibid.,* p. 16.

87 per cent of the Oregon population in the age brackets of 40 to 44 were married.[16]

Proudfoot did a comparative analysis of the characteristics of school board members as presented by various researchers.[17] His analysis shows that the range of the percentage of board members coming from professional, technical, and managerial positions was from 40 per cent in Wood's study in West Virginia to 69 per cent in Brown's 1951 study that covered the entire United States.

The percentage of school board members with some college education ranged from 33 per cent in the N.E.A. study of 1946 covering the entire United States to 72 per cent in Albert's study of 1958. These data omitted the 25 per cent from Alberta since that percentage did not include the number of school board members who had attended non-degree-granting institutions.

The mean income of board members ranged from $4,000 in Counts' study in 1927 (which would probably be close to double in terms of 1960 dollars) to $12,000 cited by Reber in California in 1959. The percentage of male board members discovered ranged from 82 per cent in Albert's study in 1958, covering the entire United States, to 98 per cent in Wood's study in 1954 in West Virginia. Albert's study in 1958 showed that the percentage of women on boards increased from 14 per cent in 1945 to 18 per cent in 1958 for the entire United States.

The average number of years served on the school board ranged from 4.1 in Counts' study in 1927 to 8.5 years in Wood's study in West Virginia in 1954. The median age of school board members ranged from 42.5 years in Tiedt and Garmire's study in Oregon to 53.4 years in Wood's study in West Virginia. Finally, the percentage of members with children in school ranged from 49 per cent in West Virginia to 92 per cent in Tiedt and Garmire's 1961 study in Oregon.

The evidence indicates that school board members tend to come from the sociologically higher occupational categories and that they tend to be in above-average occupational positions and levels of income. Counts was particularly concerned because of the lack of

[16] *Ibid.*, pp. 7–8.

[17] Alexander Proudfoot, *A Study of the Socio-Economic Status of Influential School Board Members in Alberta as Related to Their Attitudes Toward Certain Common Problems Confronting School Boards* (Unpublished Ed.D. dissertation, University of Oregon, 1962).

TABLE 2

CHARACTERISTICS OF SCHOOL BOARD MEMBERS

Author	Year of Study	Geographic Area Represented	Percentage of Board Members in Professional, Technical, or Managerial Positions	Percentage of Board with Some College Education	Mean Income of Board Members	Percentage of Male Board Members	Average Years on School Board	Median Age	Percentage of Members with Children in School
Counts	1927	United States	55	50	$ 4,000	85	4.1	48.3	—‡
N.E.A.	1946	United States	43	33	—‡	90	6.7	48.5	—‡
Brown	1951	United States	69	67	9,000	86	—‡	—‡	53
Woods	1954	West Virginia	40	26	4,250	98	8.5	53.4	49
Coughran	1956	Illinois	66	50	—‡	93	6.0	49.0	50
Teal	1956	Pennsylvania	50	50	6,000	—‡	7.0	47.5	50
Albert	1958	United States	52	72	11,968	82	6.0	48.6	70
Reber	1959	California	66	—‡	12,000	83	5.0	47.5	80
Tiedt-Garmire	1961	Oregon	61	63	9,000	91	4.7	42.5	92
Proudfoot	1962	Alberta, Canada	44	25*	6,900†	94	4.5	45.8	80

* This figure does not include attendance at non-degree-granting institutions.
† Median, not the mean, income.
‡ Data were not obtained on this item.

Source: Proudfoot, *op. cit.*

Counts, *op. cit.*

National Education Association, *op. cit.*

Brown, *op. cit.*

Roy C. Woods, "The West Virginia School Board Member," *American School Board Journal,* 128 (April, 1954), pp. 31-33.

Roy W. Coughran, *A Study of the Socio-Economic Background and the Attitudes of Illinois Public School Board Members* (Unpublished Ph.D. dissertation, Northwestern University, 1956).

Hal C. Teal, *Attitudes of Selected School Board Members Concerning Problems Facing Public Education* (Unpublished Ph.D. dissertation, University of Pittsburgh, 1956).

Albert, *op. cit.*

Donald David Reber, *A Study of the Social Composition and Attitudes of California School Board Members* (Unpublished Ed.D. dissertation, University of California at Los Angeles, 1958).

Tiedt-Garmire, *op. cit.*

labor representation on school boards. Form studied this particular problem in one Midwestern community in relationship to the total political representation of labor in the community power structure. He found that between 1935 and 1959 only two union members had been elected to the school board out of the 50 candidates, but he also noted that of the 75 candidates during this period of time, only eleven were manual or clerical workers. Sixty-three of the 75 candidates, however, were professionals, proprietors, or managerial workers. The occupational status of one candidate was not known. In 1950, union officials decided to make a greater effort to elect candidates with a point of view favorable to labor. They decided at that time to back "liberal candidates" rather than to run their own. In that election all three candidates whom they endorsed were elected, and, subsequently, they have been able to elect three of the ten candidates whom they endorsed. Subsequent analysis, however, shows that most of the candidates for school board positions still come from the census tracts in this community which are of the highest socio-economic levels and that less than one-fifth of the candidates resided in working class neighborhoods.[18] More recently, Havighurst and Neugarten have stated that there have been some changes in the socio-economic composition of city school boards in recent years. They believe that the presence of one or two representatives of organized labor on the school board is becoming more frequent. They do not, however, cite the evidence upon which this conclusion is based.[19]

The Political, Social, and Economic
Attitudes of School Board Members

The questions inevitably arise as to whether or not the social, political, and economic attitudes of school board members are reflective of a very narrow social class and whether or not school board members represent a conservative point of view which legitimizes in the schools a set of values that are congenial only to a particular segment of society. Counts feared that this was the case

---

[18] William H. Form, "Organized Labor's Place in the Community Power Structure," *Democracy in Urban America*, eds. Oliver P. Williams and Charles Press (Chicago: Rand McNally & Co., 1961), 336–38.

[19] Robert J. Havighurst and Bernice L. Neugarten, *Society in Education*, 2nd ed. (Boston: Allyn and Bacon, Inc., 1962), p. 278.

and that democracy was endangered as a result of the narrow set of values reflected by school board members. Counts' study, however, did not explore the actual values of individuals. He looked upon them merely as representatives of the class from which they came and assumed their values were the same. There is, however, some evidence to allay Counts' fears. Hunter felt that the values exemplified by school board members in Louisiana did not reflect the narrow values of any particular social class, although both their maturity and economic positions tended to make them conservative.[20] Garmire found that 64.2 per cent of the school board members in the Willamette Valley were Republicans, that 23.9 per cent were Democrats, and that 11.9 per cent indicated that they were independent. The general population in Oregon registers approximately 52 per cent Democratic.[21]

Garmire also administered the so-called liberal-conservative scale which is based on Rossiter's definition of a liberal as an individual who seeks to maintain liberty through increasing the scope of central government, while the conservative is an individual who believes that the only method of preserving liberty is to confine the size and scope of central government to its historic role.[22] On this scale the responses of the majority of school board members tended toward conservatism.[23]

Tiedt administered a number of different scales to his population, and the findings reinforced the previous studies which showed the conservative attitudes of school board members on social, political, and economic issues. On educational values, however, he found that school board members were fairly evenly distributed along the entire scale. Ninety per cent of the respondents showed a high degree of satisfaction with their present instructional programs, and 87 per cent of the board members felt that schools today do a better job than formerly. Tiedt concluded that school board members are more complex in their values and beliefs than many writers in the field have assumed.

An analysis of his data showed that there is an inconsistency in their social, political, and economic beliefs and in their edu-

---

[20] Hunter, *op. cit.*

[21] Garmire, *op. cit.*, p. 5.

[22] Clinton Rossiter, *Conservatism in America* (New York: Alfred A. Knopf, Inc., 1955), pp. 55–62.

[23] Garmire, *op. cit.*, p. 24.

cational beliefs. Tiedt points out that one cannot safely predict school board members' values with respect to education on the basis of what he knows about their political values. The evidence shows that on a general political, economic, and social scale school board members tend toward a "conservative" point of view, but with respect to the social functions of education, the extension of educational values, and educational experimentation, they tend toward a more "liberal" point of view. Tiedt concludes that "board members must, therefore, be considered as individuals rather than stereotypes if one is to gain understanding of this group."[24] An interesting finding was that school board members ranked high on the authoritarian scale, which would indicate a low tolerance for social change. With respect to their beliefs on curriculum, however, Tiedt found that school board members were generally amenable to instructional change or, in other words, more flexible in this aspect of their belief system than in their social, political, and economic opinions.

Tiedt's findings are in accord with a generalization made by Havighurst and Neugarten, who conclude on a basis of their review of some evidence that school board members have attempted to represent the entire community and that there is little if any relationship between their socio-economic beliefs and their attitudes toward the improvement of education. They suggest, in fact, that a negative correlation might exist since the higher educational and occupational levels of contemporary school board members might well be associated with relatively liberal attitudes toward the educational function.[25]

Garmire gives some clues as to why this inconsistency exists. He discovered that school board members viewed their position as a civic office in which politics or partisanship should not be evident. They saw themselves and other school board members as accepting the responsibility of office for altruistic reasons, and they believed that service on the school board constituted one of the most important civic responsibilities which a citizen could undertake. Garmire found a considerable amount of satisfaction among school board members with their service. In spite of potential conflict, school board members seem to feel that they are engaged in a very

24 Tiedt, op. cit., p. 16.
25 Havighurst and Neugarten, op. cit., pp. 278–79.

important social service that results in benefits both to the community and to the children. School board members associated a high prestige with their service on the board, even though the general community evaluation of the office placed it in a lower category of prestige.[26]

The conclusion that school board members are predominantly politically conservative cannot be contested, and as the evidence presented in Chapter II suggests, school board members tend to be elected to office because of the extent to which they represent values harmonious with the most influential elements of the community. The primary point of disagreement with previous interpretations, however, is the former assumption that this conservatism is equally apparent in their attitudes toward education as well as in other social, political, and economic concerns.

Older studies tend to express this point of view. Hollingshead, for instance, stated that the personal interviews with the members of the board of education showed that for more than a generation the school board at Elmtown had been concerned primarily with the economic operation of the schools and the promotion of conservative values in the school program. He added that board members believed that the school program should reflect "all that is traditionally good and wholesome in middle western American small town life—if it did not cost too much."[27]

Although Hollingshead asserted that school board members were constantly faced with the dilemma of educational values in opposition to cost, he nevertheless asserted that the board members were interested in seeing that everyone who could profit by a high school education was provided with the necessary facilities, although they could not clearly define the criteria by which they would appraise whether or not a student could profit from high school. Hollingshead concluded that "the members of the board had a highly developed sense of responsibility for the preservation of the economic power and prestige interest" of the upper socio-economic classes.[28]

Goldhammer, too, concluded on the basis of his investigation that although school board members felt that they represented a "com-

---

[26] Garmire, op. cit., p. 13.
[27] August B. Hollingshead, Elmtown's Youth (New York: Science Editions, 1961), pp. 124–25. It should be noted that this study was first published in 1949.
[28] Ibid., p. 125.

munity," a careful examination of their contacts and perspectives led to the conclusion that they represented only a segment of it. He found that school board members were anchored in the interests, values, and perspectives of groups in which their own socio-economic concepts provided common acceptance. For the most part, minority groups failed to achieve consistent representation, and their interests were frequently looked upon either as hostile or unimportant. He also discovered that the conservative political, social, and economic philosophy of the members of the board were reflected in the nature of the decisions which they made, but in their interviews with him school board members reflected a deep concern for the development of an educational program that would realistically meet the needs of the community and its youth.[29]

During the last decade, serious efforts have been made to improve the quality of school board membership through the development of school board associations, clinics, and in-service training programs for school board members. There can be little doubt that these programs have had a desirable effect upon the quality of school board membership. It is also apparent that qualified persons are increasingly attracted to school boards. A recent study by the United States Office of Education showed that almost half of the school board members in 1960 were college graduates.[30] Although their educational philosophies and values may to some extent conflict with those of professional educators, there is a growing tendency among school board members to view their responsibilities as an important social service and to develop a strong commitment to the disinterested improvement of the educational function for all elements of society.

---

[29] Goldhammer, "Community Power Structure and School Board Membership."

[30] *Education, U.S.A.* (October 11, 1962). Published by The National School Public Relations Association in cooperation with the Division of Press, Radio and Television Relations of the National Education Association.

CHAPTER VII

The Future of the American School Board

Serving the Public Interest

In presenting his recommendations for the improvement of public secondary education, James B. Conant stated that the first essential for a good high school, providing it is large enough to offer a satisfactory range of courses, is for the community to have "a school board composed of intelligent, understanding citizens who realize fully the *distinction between policy-making and administration*."[1] One can certainly agree with Dr. Conant that a dedicated and informed board of education is a requisite for a school program which exemplifies the characteristics of excellence so important to contemporary society. One is inclined to question, however, whether he has fully identified the most crucial problem for the operation of the school board in the modern school organization.

As previously indicated, the professional literature on school board relationships is replete with admonitions for the board to limit its duties to policy-making and to reserve all managerial functions for the professional administrative staff. Nowhere in the literature is this distinction sufficiently defined to provide the guidelines which can help individual school boards determine their operating procedures. Although one can agree with the general principle of the division, there are times when things go wrong in the school organization, when the mandates of the board are not carried out, or when the public interest is poorly served. The members of the school board then have not only the responsibility but also the obligation to their trust to enter into administrative concerns and help establish procedures which are both effective and tolerable.

In spite of Conant's identification of a major problem and clear analysis of the complexities involved in its application, it seems as

---

[1] James Bryant Conant, *The American High School Today* (New York: McGraw-Hill Book Company, 1959), p. 43.

99

though a school board might still have considerable difficulty in knowing where to draw the line. It is possible, however, for a school board to define its duties without becoming involved in major theoretical concerns which make it difficult to establish satisfactory relationships with professional personnel.

The board has the responsibility for representing the public's interest in public education and for establishing the conditions under which the school organization can operate effectively. The school board has a right and an obligation to be concerned about every aspect of the school's operation. The issue is not what should concern the board, but how it can best serve the interests of the community while making maximum use of the professional competencies which are available to it.

Rather than being primarily concerned with attempting to distinguish between policy making and administration, the school board and administrator could better use their efforts to agree upon certain behavorial interpretations of their respective roles and upon how they can work together as a team.

The board of education in an efficiently organized school district has five major areas of responsibility. It can define its duties behaviorally while it delegates to its administrative staff responsibilities which are coordinate with its own. These areas of responsibility are:

1. *The determination of major goals.*   A healthy decentralization of responsibility for certain governmental functions, including education, exists in a democratic society for the purpose of maintaining these functions close to the wishes and aspirations of the population. No central agency, under the circumstances, can define in detail the goals which should be pursued in a social function. The goals must be defined within a framework established by law and in accordance with the local population's understanding of how their efforts relate to the accomplishment of major objectives of the broader society. In this respect, decentralization can become a means for obtaining involvement and commitment of all segments of society in the effort to achieve its major social goals.

It is the function of the school board, acting on the advice of its professional staff and after careful study of the imperatives of the social scene, to determine the ends that should be served by public education, the extent to which various programs will be provided, the extension of educational programs downward below the first grade and upward beyond the twelfth grade, the degree to which curriculum should encompass both college and non-college preparatory courses, and the degree to which specialized and general education are to be incorporated within the school. These are issues which should be discussed by the school board and clearly delineated as a part of the local school's responsibility both toward its children and youth and toward the major goals of society. These policies give direction to the administrative staff who must implement, through the development of precise curriculums and learning experiences, the statement of goals established by the school board. A clear statement of goals and principles is not an academic exercise; it is a statement of the criteria upon which the schools will be evaluated.

2. *General formulation of operating policies.* The public school enterprise is a vital concern of the people in the community. As such, it is their representatives who should formulate the broad policies which will guide the management of that enterprise. Policies relating to matters that are of concern both to the curricular and noncurricular aspects of the program should be determined by the school board. The school board in this respect should draw a careful distinction between what is a matter of public policy and what is a concern that involves technical professional competency.

For example, on the advice of its superintendent the school board should decide whether or not to offer remedial reading courses in high school. The extent to which a society can afford to have individuals who have less than a fourth grade reading ability represented in adult society when their capacity is to read beyond this level is a concern of the public and one that should be decided upon in accordance with whether or not it is a worthwhile utilization of public resources to correct this deficiency. But the determination of the nature of the remedial reading program in the high school curriculum involves certain professional knowledge, and to teach remedial reading involves professional competency. The board should be concerned that the best professional knowledge available is utilized in carrying out the policy that it selects. But its decision on policy matters should relate to the public interest, and not to the technical aspects for which specially trained personnel are employed.

3. *The selection of key personnel.*   Legally, the board is responsible for the employment of all personnel within the school system. In actual practice, however, the selection of teachers and classified personnel is a technical job that must be accomplished by individuals who are especially prepared for the responsibility. The board's primary responsibility should be the selection of a competent superintendent of schools who has (1) the breadth of experience and preparation necessary to perform the services in accordance with the best professional knowledge available and (2) a concern for a proper consideration of the public interest in the management of public education.

Other key personnel who form the essential positions in relationship to the superintendent should also be carefully appraised by the school board, after they have been nominated by the superintendent, to make sure that the superintendent and his chief associates form a team that can adequately carry out the direction and management of the school organization. All other personnel must be passed upon by the school board, which should consider only personnel who are nominated by the superintendent of schools.

4. *Resource procurement and allocation.*   Since colonial times, a major concern of the people in this country has been over their proper representation in the determination of the amount of taxes which shall be levied and how these taxes shall be utilized. This function is closely related to the establishment of goals, because the public board of education is responsible for selecting those particular programs for which tax money can be allocated.

One of the serious problems confronting public education appears to be the fact that in many communities the boards of education have abrogated their obligations for the procurement of financial resources to the professional staff, who are solely responsible for "selling" tax and bond levies to the general public. An understanding of the financial structure of the schools, of the financial needs of the school district, and the manner in which the financial and other resources of the public schools are allocated and distributed is a major responsibility of the school board member. It is his duty to be able to inform the public of how their money is being spent and of how educational goals are being achieved.

5. *Evaluation.*   Any large-scale enterprise needs constantly to be evaluated to see that it is efficiently, effectively, and economically

achieving the goals for which it is established. The school board, as
Conant recommends, should not determine the curriculum, but
among other things it should constantly have evaluations of the
curriculum and of all other phases of the schools' operations presented to it. If this is done, it can appropriately determine the extent
to which the interests of the community are being well-served and
the degree to which community needs for education are being met.
The school board should expect during the course of the year that
every phase of the schools' operations will be evaluated by the professional staff. Written evaluations should be presented to the board
so that it can most adequately represent the public's interest in the
maintenance of both quality and economy in public education.

Each of these functions indicates certain things that the board
can do to improve its own procedure to guide and to evaluate the
operation of the public school program. In each instance, the school
board is not alone, since it needs the professional assistance of a
superintendent and his staff members. As a result of the actions
which it takes, the policies which it determines, and the goals which
it establishes, it imposes certain obligations for performance upon
those individuals who are professionally prepared to maintain the
day-to-day operations.

Combining Local Control and
Local Responsibility

The issue of local control for public education is still not settled,
nor will it be settled in the foreseeable future. There are those who
will continue to look upon local control as a needless decentralization of the goal-setting and policy-determining functions. They see
the results of local control as inefficiency of operations and ineffectiveness of programs. Their claims are that the conservatism of
American school board members and their too great reliance upon
criteria of economy rather than of program adequacy inevitably
results in a parsimonious provision of resources for public education and a resultant inability of the public schools to achieve the
important purposes for which they are established.

The proponents of local control believe that the ends of public
education and of democratic society will best be served to the extent
that local citizens play a reasonable part in establishing the goals

and the policies for the public schools which their children attend
and which their tax dollars help to support. They contend that cen-
tralization will stifle initiative and creativity, as it has in many for-
eign lands, and that the adaptability of the American educational
enterprise to changing social needs has been demonstrated and is
the result of the flexibility of policy determination on the local
level. They point with pride to the fact that American education has
consistently met the challenges which have confronted it and that
not only the educational programs within the public schools but
also the very governments of public education have served as a
laboratory in which the citizens learn and practice the techniques
of living in a democracy.

Although certainly under attack, the principle of local control of
education has much to commend it. There are ways in which it
can be made to function better in order to serve the needs of a
vigorous and demanding public.

1. *A new definition of the relationship of local control to cen-
tralization needs to be established.* As long as local control leads
to local irresponsibility with respect to the provision of the resources
needed to maintain the quality of education, the critics of local control will find many examples of how communities fail to bear their
responsibilities for promoting the national interest. As long as
school boards place local parochial interests before national needs
and the requirements of the broader society, local control imposes
a barrier to both the proper defense and the full development of
society. But the community and the nation are not in conflict; the
child lives in both and needs educational experiences which adequately prepare him for living in both. Board members and administrators must recognize this fact and make it a criterion upon
which their decisions are made.

Communities differ in their levels of aspiration for the education
of their children. Some communities still fail to recognize the significant social changes that have taken place in society and the types
of competition their children will face as they leave the community
to seek employment. Some communities are guided by economic
interests that are indifferent to anything but their local concerns.
National and state constitutions almost invariably include provisions for the government's protection of the rights of individuals
against lower subdivisions which may infringe upon them. The

courts have recognized the obligations of state governments, in particular, to establish legislation to protect the rights and the welfare of dependent and legally incompetent groups in society. Because of this responsibility, it is the obligation of the state legislators, through the state board of education and the state department of education, to establish the standards under which local schools shall be operated. Such standards define the minimum programs and conditions which must prevail. They guarantee at least a modicum of equality of educational opportunity for all children in the state. They protect children from the capricious and irresponsible decisions of adults who may be swayed by temporal aspirations and fears. They prescribe the extent to which every community shall participate in the national effort to protect and preserve this country's democratic heritage. Rather than restricting local control, they establish the rules governing the effective decision making on the local level and help make local control synonymous with local responsibility. They establish the principle of the partnership of the state and the community in promoting the welfare and interest of both.

2. Consistent with this point of view, *a broader perspective of what constitutes the school district needs also to be established.* Many authorities, after careful study of public education in the various parts of the United States, have agreed that the most serious problem facing public education during the last half of the twentieth century is the proper reorganization of school districts. Various studies have consistently shown that smaller school districts are not only uneconomical but also that they result in an inferior education and a failure fully to develop the human resources needed both for defense and civilian maintenance of our society.

The small rural elementary school district with less than one teacher for each grade, or a high school with less than three hundred pupils, was an answer to the educational needs of society when transportation and communication were relatively primitive. With the modern means of rapid communication and transportation and the network of adequate roads throughout most parts of the United States, the small village school is no longer tolerable, and responsible policy making on the local level means that the educational community must be conceived as no less than that size which is sufficient to maintain an educational program which is entirely adequate for all the children and youth of this nation. Many states have already embarked on a vigorous reorganization of school districts, primarily in the interests of improving their programs and demonstrating their responsibility for meeting the educational requirements of the nation, and secondarily, in order to make a more efficient and effective utilization of scarce tax dollars.

3. In the decades ahead, in order to make local control work under changing social conditions, *there needs to be a broader public participation in the affairs of the school.* Studies have consistently shown that some segments of the community are denied access to membership on school boards because powerful and influential elements in the community attempt to control school board membership and to promote ends or maintain values which they deem important. To broaden the base for decision making and participation in local affairs will enhance the ability of school boards to demonstrate that local control can be truly representative in governing American public education. At the same time, they and the schools can serve the interests of all the people. They will demonstrate that local communities can make democracy work.

4. As society has become more complex and as school districts have grown in size, school boards have become increasingly divorced from the public whom they represent in the management of public education. To regain some of the public control which should characterize local control over public education and to make the decision making of public education better serve the function of providing a laboratory for the practice of democratic citizenship, *additional citizens' groups within the community should be incorporated within the decision-making structure of the school board.* On important decisions, school boards should employ techniques such as citizens' advisory committees to aid them in gaining a broader perspective of the opinions and reactions of qualified persons within the community, to utilize specialized knowledge and understandings that are available within the community, and to enable more people to express their concerns so that increasingly better decisions can be made.

5. *The decision-making techniques of school boards need to be studied* so that each school board endeavors to seek out those policies that are most valuable, not on the basis of opinion or mere preference, but by utilizing careful techniques of investigation and

inquiry to determine the pertinent facts, the potential alternatives of action, and the possible consequences of the various decisions that can be made. The decision-making process should become an empirical search for the general principles which will be most likely to serve the best interests of the community.

6. *Board members should constantly seek to improve their ability to perform their duties, both as members of the school board and as citizens of the community.* Board members should avail them-selves of opportunities to participate in school board association meetings, in-service training programs, clinics, and school board conferences. One of the reasons for the significant improvement of public education during the last decade has been the degree to which the quality of school board membership has been upgraded. It is necessary constantly to upgrade and improve the contributions which each school board member makes to his community and to the furtherance of the educational program of the public schools.

7. Consistent with the discussion in the previous section, *it is necessary for the board to maintain proper definitions of the shared responsibilities which exist between the citizen board and the pro-fessional staff.* Because of diverse backgrounds, it is always possible for school board members and educators to enter into conflict and to guard prerogatives from one another in the fear that one is usurp-ing the proper functions of the other. When conflict, misunderstand-ing, and jealousy arise, the interests of education are ill-served. It is constantly desirable for board members and professional educa-tors to bear in mind that they both serve the education of the chil-dren and the promotion of the worthwhile social goals of society. Their contributions can be effective only to the extent that they share their responsibility and work together as a team in a con-sistent fashion.

Bibliography

American Association of School Administrators, *School Board-Superintend-ent Relationships*. Washington, D.C.: The Association, 1956.

Brown, R. A., "Composition of School Boards," *American School Board Journal*, 129 (August, 1954), 23–24.

Carter, Richard F., *Voters and Their Schools*. Stanford, Calif.: Stanford University Press, 1960.

Conant, James Bryant, *The American High School Today*. New York: Mc-Graw-Hill Book Company, 1959.

Cunningham, Luvern L., "Decision-Making Behavior of School Boards," *American School Board Journal*, 144 (February, 1962), 13–16.

Davies, Daniel R., "School Boards for Tomorrow," *National Education Association Journal*, 38 (January, 1950), 18–19.

Edwards, Newton, *The Courts and The Public Schools*, rev. ed. Chicago: University of Chicago Press, 1955.

Foskett, John M., "Social Structure and Social Participation," *American Sociological Review*, 20 (August, 1955), 431–48.

————, "Local Control: Folklore and Obsolescence," *American School Board Journal*, 142 (May, 1961), 40–42.

Garber, Lee B., *The Yearbook of School Law*. Danville, Ill.: Interstate Publishers, 1962. Published annually since 1955.

Garmire, Leonard, "A Study of the Attitudes of School Board Members As They Relate to Reasons for Seeking Office," *Oregon School Study Council Bulletin*, Vol. 6, No. 2. Eugene, Oregon: The School of Education, University of Oregon, 1962.

Goldhammer, Keith, "The School Board and Administration in the American Perspective of Government," *American School Board Journal*, 129 (November, 1954), 29–31 and (December, 1954), 29–30.

————, "Community Power Structure and School Board Membership," *American School Board Journal*, 130 (March, 1955), 23–25.

————, "The Administrator and His Community," *American School Board Journal*, 134 (May, 1957), 35–36.

————, "The Administration of the Community's Schools," *American School Board Journal*, 139 (October, 1959), 27–30.

Goldhammer, Keith and Lloyd Cooper, "A Survey of the Definition of School Board Powers," *Oregon School Study Council Bulletin*, Vol. 4, No. 8. Eugene, Oregon: The School of Education, University of Oregon, 1961.

Griffiths, Daniel E., *Human Relations in School Administration*. New York: Appleton-Century-Crofts, Inc., 1956.

Gross, Neal, *Who Runs Our Schools?* New York: John Wiley & Sons, Inc., 1958.

Hall, Morill M., *Provisions Governing Membership on Local Boards of Education*, Bulletin No. 3. Washington, D.C.: Department of Health, Education, and Welfare, 1957.

Hamilton, Robert R. and E. Edmund Reutter, *Legal Aspects of School Board Operation*. New York: Bureau of Publications, Teachers College, Columbia University, 1958.

Hamilton, Robert R. and Paul R. Mort, *The Law and Public Education*. New York: The Foundation Press, 1959.

Hines, Clarence, "A Study of School Board Administrative Relationships: The Development of the Eugene, Oregon, Superintendency, 1891–1944," *American School Board Journal*, 122 (February, 1951), 14–21; (March, 1951), 28–29; (April, 1951), 17–19.

Hollingshead, August B., *Elmtown's Youth*. New York: Science Editions, 1961.

Knill, William, "Who Censure the Public Schools?" *Oregon School Study Council Bulletin*, Vol. 4, No. 9. Eugene, Oregon: The School of Education, University of Oregon, 1961.

Lieberman, Myron, *The Future of Public Education*. Chicago: University of Chicago Press, 1960.

Reeves, Charles E., *School Boards*. Englewood Cliffs, N.J.: Prentice-Hall, Inc., 1954.

Remmlein, M. K., "Legal Status of Local School Boards," *American School Board Journal*, 125 (May–June, 1952), 25–27.

Smith, Max S. and W. Roy Smittle, *The Board of Education and Educational Policy Development*. Ann Arbor, Mich.: Edwards Brothers, 1954.

Stapley, Maurice E., *School Board Studies*. Chicago: Midwest Administration Center, 1957.

Tiedt, Sidney W., "Oregon School Board Members in the Willamette Valley," *Oregon School Study Council Bulletin*, Vol. 6, No. 6. Eugene, Oregon: The School of Education, University of Oregon, 1962.

Tucker, Cecil I., "The School Board's Decisions," *The University of South Carolina Education Report*, Vol. V, No. 4 (April, 1962).

Vidich, Arthur J. and Joseph Bensman, *Small Town in Mass Society*. Princeton, N.J.: Princeton University Press, 1958.

Walton, John, *Administration and Policy-Making In Education*. Baltimore: Johns Hopkins Press, 1959.

Index